I0867581

This is number one hundred and ninety-one
in the second numbered series of the
Miegunyah Volumes
made possible by the
Miegunyah Fund
established by bequests
under the wills of
Sir Russell and Lady Grimwade.

'Miegunyah' was Russell Grimwade's home
from 1911 to 1955
and Mab Grimwade's home
from 1911 to 1973.

Historian Stuart Kells has twice won the Ashurst Business Literature Prize, and has been shortlisted for the Prime Minister's Literary Award, the NSW Premier's General History Prize and the University of Queensland Non-Fiction Book Award. Kells' shorter pieces have appeared in *The Paris Review*, *The Times*, *Lapham's Quarterly*, *Smithsonian*, *The Guardian*, *National Geographic Traveller* and *The Daily Beast*. He is Adjunct Professor at La Trobe University's College of Arts, Social Sciences and Commerce, and a member of the Abbotsford Convent Foundation Board.

THE CONVENT

A city finds its Heart

Stuart Kells

THE MIEGUNYAH PRESS

THE MIEGUNYAH PRESS
An imprint of Melbourne University Publishing Limited
Level 1, 715 Swanston Street, Carlton, Victoria 3053, Australia
mup-contact@unimelb.edu.au
www.mup.com.au

First published 2020

This book has been produced with the generous support and participation of the Public Record Office Victoria, the Wurundjeri Woi Wurrung Cultural Heritage Aboriginal Corporation, the Abbotsford Convent Foundation and the Lane Press.

For further information on the Abbotsford Convent's history, visit abbotsfordconvent.com.au

Cover design by Pfisterer + Freeman
Typeset in 11/15pt New Caledonia by Cannon Typesetting
Printed in Australia by McPherson's Printing Group

NATIONAL LIBRARY OF AUSTRALIA
A catalogue record for this book is available from the National Library of Australia

9780522876598 (paperback)
9780522876604 (ebook)

For Patricia O'Donnell (1945–2018)

Contents

Acknowledgements

The research and writing of this book was supported by a Local History Grant from the Public Record Office Victoria, and I gratefully acknowledge that support.

Attempting to write a history of the Abbotsford Convent, and particularly a record of the community campaign to save the convent grounds and buildings from commercial development, was always going to be a collective endeavour. This book reflects the generous guidance and input of many interviewees and correspondents over the span of more than two years. I acknowledge and thank in particular Aunty Gail, Aunty Julieanne and other members of the Wurundjeri Woi Wurrung Cultural Heritage Aboriginal Corporation; Sister Monica Walsh, Sister Barbara Walsh, Kathy Landvogt and Fraser Faithfull of the Good Shepherd; Susan Bannerman, Jo Kinross, Tony Lee, Charlotte Allen, Margot Foster, Hilary Rankin, Sally Romanes, Nigel Lewis and other former members of the Abbotsford Convent Coalition and affiliated organisations; Michelle Quigley; Robert Pradolin; Catherine Kovesi; Bill Russell, Hayden Raysmith, Mike Smith, Victoria Marles, Maggie Maguire, Collette Brennan, Jacqueline Hanlin and other former and current members of the Abbotsford Convent Foundation (ACF) Board and the ACF team; Councillor Amanda Stone and other former and current members of Yarra City Council; the Hon. Steve Bracks, the Hon. Richard Wynne, MP, the Hon. Mary Delahunty and other former and current members of the Victorian parliament and the Victorian government; La Trobe University and the University of Melbourne.

It is a matter of great sadness for the Abbotsford Convent community that Patricia O'Donnell, much-loved friend and patron of the arts, died on 16 October 2018. Patricia played a crucial role in the community campaign, and then as a strategist and mentor who helped shape the convent as a viable and vibrant arts organisation. I had the wonderful privilege of serving on the ACF board alongside Patricia, and of interviewing her and hearing her stories in the preparation of this book.

In tracing the history of the convent, I was also guided by prior authors and researchers, most notably Dr Catherine Kovesi, whose *Pitch Your Tents on Distant Shores* is the definitive history of the Sisters of the Good Shepherd in Australia.

Marvellous and extensive archives of the Abbotsford Convent are held at the State Library of Victoria, the Good Shepherd and Tony Lee's home, and I had generous access to these invaluable resources.

My wife, Fiona Kells, helped find key documents, assisted with referencing, read multiple drafts of the manuscript, and otherwise assisted in dozens of practical and essential ways. I thank Fiona for her help and support on this and other projects. Our daughters, Thea and Charlotte, also deserve thanks for their practical help and forbearance.

Louise Lane of the Lane Press was another crucial member of the team behind the book. She assisted with project management, the interviews and archival research, and the planning of the book itself. Louise has been for me a valued and trusted guide.

The team at Melbourne University Publishing turned the manuscript into a crisp and handsome book. I thank in particular MUP's Cathryn Smith, David Lawlor, editor extraordinaire Katie Purvis, and designers Pfisterer + Freeman.

For tens of thousands of years, Indigenous Australians owned the Abbotsford peninsula and surrounding country. I acknowledge that continuity of ownership and culture, and the crimes and dispossession experienced by the Traditional Owners.

Finally, I acknowledge the history and stories of the women and girls who worked and resided at the convent during its time as a working monastic site, from 1863 until 1975, run by the Order of the Sisters of the Good Shepherd at Abbotsford.

In 2009, the Sisters of the Good Shepherd formally recognised and acknowledged that the conditions within the order's institutions were tough and isolating for many people. The Sisters of the Good Shepherd apologised to the people who experienced mistreatment and neglect while in the sisters' care.

The sisters also supported the Australian Royal Commission into Institutional Responses to Child Sexual Abuse, which helped give survivors a voice and brought to light aspects of their experiences and ongoing suffering.

This book captures elements and instances of the experiences of nuns, novices, residents, penitents, inmates, wards, orphans and students within the convent, but it is not a complete record of those experiences or the daily suffering and hardship that many people endured. The full story of those experiences remains to be told, and there is much healing still to be done.

Professor Stuart Kells

1
A secret, magical place

WHAT WAS BEHIND the wall and the wire? The local people knew. A cluster of large and handsome buildings, most of them built in the Gothic style before World War I and all of them now resembling an abandoned medieval French village. There were fine courtyards, too, and an old swimming pool, and dilapidated tennis courts, and a remnant garden—once grand and kempt, now wild and sprawling. One of the largest trees was a venerable oak, planted almost 150 years ago. An arc of overgrown meadows connected the buildings and the garden to the banks of a sweeping bend in the Yarra River.

From time to time the locals ventured through cracks in the wall or gaps in the wire. They took cuttings from the garden's unruly roses and seedlings of its rare tomatoes. They picnicked in the grounds and the riverside meadows, finding refuge in the remarkable quiet that was broken only by the uncanny ring of bellbirds. The most adventurous visitors invaded the old buildings or played clandestine games of twilight tennis on the derelict courts.

This mysterious site occupied a heart-shaped peninsula that was bounded by the Yarra to the south-west, the south-east and the north-east. The opposite bank was steep and heavily wooded, mostly with tall eucalypts, but also wattles and other native trees and shrubs: a striking semicircle of urban bushland just 4 kilometres from the centre of a large city.

Covered walkways, stained glass, a fine chapel, a solemn cloister. These and other features of the buildings and grounds gave away their former life. The site had once housed a busy religious community: the Convent of the Order of the Good Shepherd. Now, though, the nuns and their wards had gone and the site had been reduced to a kind of inner-urban land bank, suspended in time, lost in the too-hard basket.

Central Melbourne may have been nearby, but the peninsula felt a million miles from Collins and Bourke streets. Families and school groups visited the neighbouring Children's Farm—formerly the convent's larder—to meet goats and rabbits and peacocks. Cyclists and runners sped by on the recently opened riverside bike path. People from the neighbourhood walked dogs and took strolls. Otherwise, there was little passing traffic.

Margot Foster was one passer-by. A producer at ABC Radio National, she lived in William Street, a few blocks from the old convent site. In 1997 she was walking with her son and her dog along St Heliers Street on the site's northern edge when a large sign stopped her in her tracks. Evidently the place was about to be transformed. A property developer had a new vision for the unique site's 6.7 hectares.

From 1990, the developer had traded as 'Australian Housing and Land', or 'Australand' for short. That name was somewhat misleading. In its corporate communications, the company trumpeted its Australian heritage, which extended back to 1924 with the founding of TM Burke Pty Ltd. Now, though, the company was majority owned and controlled by a Singapore government body, CapitaLand; it would soon seek a dual listing on the Australian and Singaporean stock exchanges.

According to the Australand vision, a redeveloped 'St Heliers Convent' would be an exclusive, high-density residential enclave. By remaking the old structures and pulling other ones down, and by building large new ones in the gaps and around the edges, Australand would create 289 residential units. One of the proposed buildings, a six-storey tower, would overlook the Children's Farm and the river. The other buildings included rows of three- and four-storey townhouses along the riverside path. Several existing buildings would retain just their facades. Vaunted features of the redevelopment proposal included a boat landing and a four-hole 'chip-and-putt' golf course, slated for the French Meadow.

This kind of closed-off, high-density residential development—in which repurposed heritage buildings were blended with modern and utilitarian ones—was altering neighbourhoods across Melbourne. Big developments were changing the shape and fabric of the inner city, Southbank, South Carlton, the inner east, the inner west and the bayside suburbs. But the Australand proposal was unusual for its scale and ambition.

Amanda Stone also saw the big sign on St Heliers Street: 'Australand Is Coming'. So did Jo Kinross. Word spread about what Australand and the state government's Urban Land Authority had in mind. People in the community were eager for more information. The residents of Abbotsford and nearby suburbs wanted to understand what was happening in their neighbourhood.

In 1997, the use of email wasn't widespread and social media platforms were embryonic. The concerned residents shared information in low-tech ways, such as by letter and phone and in person. Thanks to these technologies, Abbotsford was home to a highly effective bush telegraph. With speed and efficiency, the residents swapped snippets of knowledge and the beginnings of ideas about what could and should be done. They also contacted others, in search of more information to share and act upon. Foster spoke to media colleagues. Her fellow residents put the word out among Melbourne's architects, archaeologists and conservators.

The formal planning process involved some new players. Just three years earlier, the state government had created the City of Yarra by amalgamating the former inner-suburban municipalities of Collingwood, Fitzroy and Richmond, plus parts of Carlton North, Alphington and Fairfield. Now, the new council had the job of preparing a critical document that would pave the way for Australand's redevelopment: Planning Amendment number L54.

The planning amendment process was enshrined in Victorian legislation. As part of the process, Australand's representatives had to talk to affected residents. On 24 November 1997, the developer fulfilled this requirement in the most minimal way possible. By letter drop, it notified as few as six households and businesses immediately to the west of the old convent site about the amendment process and the opportunity to attend public information briefings.

Psychologist Sue Bannerman was one of the Clarke Street residents who received a letter from Australand. She lived at number 13, 'Osborne House', built in 1864. When the letter arrived, she was at her front gate chatting to a neighbour. Bannerman looked inside the envelope and some details jumped out at her, especially the proposed ten-storey tower on the convent car park. She then read the whole letter carefully and spoke to other neighbours.

On the Sunday after Bannerman received the letter, a few people were gathered around her kitchen table to talk about what was proposed and what they might do about it when they heard a knock at the door. It was Robyn Williams, the residents' ward councillor. She didn't know Bannerman, but had heard on the grapevine that Sue's kitchen was the place to be.

Williams shared a critical piece of information. The proposed redevelopment wasn't a fait accompli. The site could be used for housing only if it received approval from the local council. The nearby residents wouldn't have to throw themselves in front of bulldozers—or at least not yet.

Williams emphasised the scale and significance of what was afoot. 'This is really important,' she said to the residents around the table. 'You have to get organised.' Then she gave them practical advice on how to do just that.

Thanks to Williams, and to the Australand briefings, the residents began to understand the gravity of the situation. The attendees at the briefings didn't like what they heard: the scale of the proposal and its likely impact on the people of eastern Abbotsford were staggering. Using the bush telegraph, they alerted as many other people as they could.

By these means, Williams and the concerned residents called a public meeting to discuss the proposed development. Five days after the Australand briefings, more than 100 people gathered on the weedy, gravelly car park at the northern edge of the convent site, between St Heliers Street and Johnston Street.

The meeting was unanimous: Australand was in La La Land and the redevelopment had to be stopped. The gathered residents resolved to launch a public campaign. They would form the St Heliers Convent Action Group, and they would do what they could to save the precious, magical, secret place that was Melbourne's green heart.

2

It began with lava

FOR MILLIONS OF years there were active volcanoes to the north and west of where Melbourne now stands. Molten lava flowed implacably outward from the volcano fields to form a basalt plain. At its south-eastern edge, the plain met ancient sandstone and mudstone and siltstone. This frontier defined the course of a river. The Yarra River.

In the last Ice Age, the Yarra was of much greater extent than it is today. Through what is now Port Phillip Bay and The Heads, it ran out to join the Barwon River and, in what would later become northern Tasmania, the Tamar. Ultimately the rising sea levels that made Tasmania also helped make the Yarra.

For the local Wurundjeri people—one of the five tribes of the Indigenous Kulin Nation—the river was of great cultural significance. The Wurundjeri tell of how two ancestral headmen, Bar-wool and Yan Yan, made the river by cutting through barriers with axes, thereby emptying a great mountain pool into the bay. Thereafter, the river was central to daily life. People drank from it and lived on its banks. When travelling, they carried Yarra water in possum-skin bags.

Over the span of tens of thousands of years, the Abbotsford peninsula was an important meeting place for the Indigenous people of south-eastern Australia. Set in a naturally enclosed amphitheatre, the peninsula was immediately downstream from an ancient crossing point near what is now Dights Falls. The region was home to many native vertebrates, including fish, platypuses, koalas, wombats, wallabies, kangaroos, echidnas, quolls, emus, blue-tongues and snakes—plus a great variety of plants. Seals and dolphins forayed upriver from the open ocean and the bay to catch fish and explore the fresher water.

Ideal for hunting and fishing and food collection, the rich river flats and deep water met many of the people's needs. On land, the Wurundjeri caught kangaroos and possums. In the water, they caught eels and bream and perch. Nothing was wasted. The people sharpened mussel shells to scrape possum skins, and used echidna quills for sewing and to make necklaces. Riverside trees were sources of seeds and resins. Riverside vines were dried and twisted to make strong and versatile rope.

The first Europeans to venture into inland Victoria also used the river. In 1802, Governor Philip Gidley King ordered Charles Grimes, the newly appointed surveyor-general of New South Wales, to survey the countryside in the immediate vicinity of Port Phillip. The surveyor's expedition was of the utmost importance as other countries besides Britain had eyes on this section of coast. The expedition would help forestall possible foreign interest in the Bass Strait area, especially from the French.

In February 1803, Grimes and James Fleming mapped vegetation and surveyed the Yarra. Fleming camped with the Wurundjeri people below the ancient crossing place and sowed seeds there. The expeditioners soon left the region, but over the following decades their countrymen would be back, and in large numbers.

The next European visitors would become household names and street names and school curriculum names: Hume and Hovell (1824), Charles Sturt (1830) and Edward Henty (1834). In 1835, fifteen citizens from Van Diemen's Land formed the Port Phillip Association (originally the Geelong and Dutigalla Association) to acquire land from the Indigenous peoples of the mainland's south-east coast. In May of that year, John Batman sailed from Launceston on the *Rebecca*. After entering Port Phillip and anchoring at Indented Head, he sailed to the mouth of the Yarra.

Soon after, the Wurundjeri headman Bebejern and seven other Indigenous leaders reportedly 'signed' Batman's 'deed of Melbourne'. The Indigenous Australian culture was a verbal one: the Indigenous signatures weren't signatures at all, and the 'deed' was unconscionably one-sided. But by this means, more than 500,000 prime, verdant and culturally redolent acres (202,000 hectares) were 'traded' for a modest bounty of blankets, flour, tomahawks, knives, scissors, looking glasses, handkerchiefs and shirts.

That same year, a misunderstanding gave the Yarra its modern name. John Wedge was Batman's surveyor. At the old falls near today's Southbank, Wedge was with some Indigenous people when they said, 'Yarra Yarra' ('Yarrow Yarrow' is what he wrote in his notebook). Only later did Wedge and others realise that the people were referring to the movement of the water over the falls, not to the river as a whole—which the people actually called *Birrarung* or *Brahrung*, the 'river of mists'.

In March 1837, Governor Sir Richard Bourke arrived at Port Phillip. Accompanying him was the surveyor Robert Hoddle. Bourke directed that a town be laid out, and appointed Hoddle as senior surveyor. By the end of April, Hoddle's plan for the new town of 'Melbourne' was lodged at the government survey office in Sydney. The centrepiece of the plan—on land about 5 kilometres from the Abbotsford peninsula—was Hoddle's iconic grid of wide streets and narrow lanes.

The following year, Hoddle and his staff surveyed both sides of the Yarra near Abbotsford and subdivided it into uniform allotments of 25 acres (10 hectares), except where natural features made uniformity impossible. In this way, Hoddle enabled the first land releases that expanded Melbourne beyond the grid-like urban centre. The allotments were sold as 'rural retreats for gentlemen' and were approved for subdivision.

Major Henry Smyth of Sydney purchased Crown portions 77 (23a) and 64 (12a), totalling 35 acres (14 hectares), on the Yarra at Abbotsford. In 1840, John Hodgson leased part of this riverside estate from Smyth. Two years later, the Hon. Isaac Erskine Murray bought Smyth's whole estate and further divided it into riverside 'farmlets'.

John Orr was a businessman, pastoral pioneer and politician. An alderman in the first Melbourne City Council of December 1842, he would also be a founding member of the Victorian parliament. In July 1842, he purchased 'Abbotsford Estate': seven picturesque acres on the Clarke Street edge of the peninsula's subdivision.

In the same year, Edward Curr purchased the neighbouring property on the peninsula's easternmost side. Curr, like Orr, was active in colonial politics. A member for the Port Phillip District in the New South Wales Legislative Council, he led the 1840s campaign to separate the district from New South Wales. Curr's property consisted of around 16 acres that were divided into orchards, ornamental gardens and a large paddock. It was here that he built a fine home, 'St Heliers'. His daughter Elizabeth, who was eight years old when she arrived in Melbourne, later wrote that St Heliers was a delightful property. She recalled that visitors from the Melbourne township 'seemed to look at the garden as a sort of promised land' and that her father acquired two roan horses and a carriage from London, which he used to travel to town for his business and political activities.

In 1843, Orr built the equally fine 'Abbotsford House'. The name harked back to the home of the Scottish novelist and poet Sir Walter Scott. In 1811, Scott had bought 'Newarthaugh', a mountain farm that sat 'on a bare haugh and bleak bank by the side of the Tweed'. The local people called the property 'Cartleyhole' or 'Clarty Hole', but Scott renamed it 'Abbotsford', 'after the ford across the Tweed below the house used in former times by the monks of Melrose Abbey'. He planted trees and extended the farmhouse, which became a 'whimsical and picturesque' building that featured a study, dining room, armoury, conservatory and library. The armoury would later serve as the author's 'boudoir'. Though less extensive and picturesque than Scott's home, Orr's 'Abbotsford' was a large house with high ceilings and a wide veranda. The grounds featured pleasant shrubberies, orchards and flower gardens.

On 11 November 1850, news reached Melbourne that the separation campaign had succeeded: Britain's parliament had passed legislation to separate the Port Phillip District from New South Wales.

Just five days later, Curr died. Obituarists credited him as the Father of Separation.

In December, Curr's trustees let out St Heliers in two parts. Robert Cole took the lower garden and paddock, while William F Lord took the house and its adjoining garden. Later in the 1850s, George Young would lease St Heliers, and Samuel Moss—an American hotelier, restaurateur and sometime playwright—would lease part of Abbotsford Estate.

Subsequent notable lessees would reportedly include Hugh Childers (Commissioner of Customs, Steam Navigation Board chairman and vice-chancellor of the University of Melbourne) and Charles W Ligar (Victoria's surveyor general). With Robert Patterson and John Mackenzie, Orr would eventually subdivide the northern part of the estate into town lots and advertise them for sale. In the early 1860s, Mr Frederick Cooke, manager of the Melbourne Banking Company, would own and occupy Abbotsford House.

3
Sue's kitchen

For a brief period in the 1850s—'the golden fifties'—this Abbotsford neighbourhood between Hoddle Street and the Yarra was an exclusive one. According to the *Williamstown Chronicle*, prosperous woolbroker Richard Goldsbrough lived there, as did 'some others of the upper class. It was then the Toorak of those days, but too many of the working class went out that way, and the "gentry" left.'

The neighbourhood they left behind became a zone of narrow streets, modest blocks and closely packed houses with meagre backyards. It was also known for its hotels of various vintages, and its warehouses and small factories: breweries, butcheries, tanneries, candle makers, textile workshops, soap factories. Apart from along the riverbank, public open space in Abbotsford was as scarce as private space in those cramped yards.

When the 1990s arrived, the old houses and factories were mostly still there. Abbotsford was noteworthy for its largely untouched streetscapes of Victorian and Edwardian worker's cottages in timber and rendered brick. The neighbourhood had a demography and a flavour that had once been widespread in inner Melbourne but was now disappearing, especially in nearby Carlton and Clifton Hill, which were rapidly gentrifying.

Economically, culturally and ethnically, Abbotsford's social geography was diverse. Retirees, families, students. People with Chinese,

Greek, Italian, Vietnamese and Anglo-Australian heritage. Alongside patches of prosperity, there were pockets of poverty. Apart from professional people, there was a strong artistic, alternative and New Age presence.

Though La Trobe University owned the old convent site, it had long entertained plans to sell it. In 1994 the state government tasked the Urban Land Authority with managing the sale process. The curious history of the ULA dated back to the 1970s and an earlier incarnation as the Urban Land Council. A Whitlam Government initiative, it was conceived in 1972 and brought into being by Victoria's Hamer Government in 1975, in response to a public scandal involving the Housing Commission and corrupt land deals.

When it was first constituted, the ULA inherited a portfolio of estates and responsibilities as well as surplus land from the government and the Housing Commission. With its new statutory mandate, it marketed land for residential and non-residential purposes and was responsible for a plethora of property developments, such as ones at Roxburgh Park, Port Melbourne and the old Hawthorn tram depot.

Wholly owned by the state government, the ULA was a public entity with official powers and direct accountability to the state parliament. But it nevertheless operated in an assertively commercial way: a public land-broker that operated more like a private stockbroker. This was the entity commissioned by the government to manage the sale of the former convent site. In 1997, the ULA called for tenders. Australand's bid was reportedly in the vicinity of $20 million—more than double the valuer-general's valuation. The ULA accepted Australand's offer subject to the rezoning of the convent land for residential use.

Opposition to Planning Amendment L54 had to follow a specified process. According to that process, objections from residents had to be submitted by Christmas Eve 1997. Armed with the advice from Robyn Williams and the resolutions from the car-park meeting, the residents got moving. They stuck signs on trees and distributed information sheets outlining what was planned and the implications for the site and for Abbotsford and Melbourne more broadly. They called on their contacts. They thought and planned. And they organised.

In December 1997, an important event took place: the newly formed St Heliers Convent Action Group had its first meeting. Four people reconvened, naturally, around the kitchen table at Sue Bannerman's house on Clarke Street: Bannerman herself, Hilary Archer (an artist), Jo Kinross (a counsellor, consultant and 'jack-of-all-trades') and Nigel Lewis (a conservation architect).

Others would soon join this core group, among them Charlotte Allen, Amanda Stone, Nicole Fraser, Anna Lindstad, Maryann Croatto, Margot Foster, Hilary Rankin, Hilary McPhee, Basil Natoli, Perry Snowden, Cassandra Tyler, and Greg Milne of the Children's Farm. Lewis would bring along Tony Lee, a heritage architect, and David Ingamells, a psychiatrist.

The majority of the campaigners were women, and nearly all were tertiary educated and in their late thirties or their forties. Collectively, they represented a diverse range of occupations and backgrounds. These were the people who were determined to do something—though they weren't sure precisely what—about the Australand proposal.

The core members of the convent campaign were all accomplished and assertive—even opinionated—but, for the most part, when they began the campaign they left their egos at the door. The first meeting around the small table set the pattern for all future gatherings: respectful, collaborative, energetic, passionate. The approach was also rigorous and professional. Right from the beginning, minutes were taken and actions and decisions recorded. This thing they were doing was only going to work if it was done properly.

From the first days of the campaign to save the convent, Kinross stood out as the residents' de facto leader and most committed member. People inside and outside the campaign would soon be referring to her as its linchpin. Agile and courageous, she was the 'glue', the 'mother superior', the 'helicopter' who could grapple with different priorities and serve on multiple battlefronts at once while keeping the end in view. 'Jo always kept her eye on the big picture,' Lee remembered.

Detecting this 'helicopter' capacity in Kinross, the *Age* newspaper would later describe her as 'terrier-like'. She was experienced in government, education, community development, counselling, the arts and other fields. Soon she would give up her day job to work full time, and without pay, on the campaign.

• • •

The residents' concerns about the Australand development proposal had multiple facets. Fears about overshadowing from the towers. Fears about excessive traffic and loss of open space. Fears about inappropriate riverside development. And fears about loss of heritage.

In 1993, the convent buildings, along with the neighbouring Children's Farm, had been placed on the Historic Buildings Register. The significance of the convent site was incontrovertible: it was the last remaining intact, inner-urban, nineteenth-century convent complex and landscape in the world. If the development went ahead as planned, the existing convent buildings would be transformed. New floors and new ceiling heights would obliterate their interiors, as would the removal of light wells and staircases and glass. Other layers of heritage were also at risk: traces of the early farmlets, and evidence of the much earlier and much longer ownership and stewardship by First Australians. A lot was at stake.

Lewis saw that the Australand proposal would destroy or conceal important internal features and structures. Historic convent buildings—such as Mercator and the Magdalen Laundry—would become gutted facades for new two- and four-storey blocks. He was also concerned about the loss of the convent's unique, largely unaltered nineteenth-century rural landscape, one that in 1803 was a site of first contact with Australia's Indigenous people, and that later became a sought-after residential location for the pioneers of the Port Phillip District.

One of the most worrying aspects of the development proposal was the loss of open space near the river. The members of the community who had made informal visits to the convent site already felt a sense of ownership over it. Now that ownership was under threat, as was the amenity that went with it. The plan to build a four-hole chip-and-putt golf course on the French Meadow felt like an especially crass trade-off. Hilary Rankin called that aspect of the Australand proposal 'alarming'.

The loss of bike-path access was another fear. The Capital City Trail bicycle route had only recently been constructed. It ran along the river and then between the convent and the farm. Though new, it had already accumulated many users and many more supporters. But under the Australand proposal, townhouses were to be built within a few metres of the path. The development would certainly encroach upon this new thoroughfare, and some residents feared they might lose access to it altogether.

The farm, too, was at risk of encroachment. For children and families from across Melbourne, it was an inner-urban oasis, a way to experience the country in the city. The campaigners pictured a future clash between the residents of an exclusive riverside enclave and the users of a small-scale, not-for-profit, community-managed children's farm. In such a clash, the action group feared, the farm would surely lose out.

Across inner Melbourne there were plenty of examples of how residents of new high-density developments had successfully objected to local live music venues, even though those venues had been there first and had long been a defining feature of their neighbourhoods. The prospect of a farm fight was even more daunting. Who would win in a battle over the noise—and the round-the-clock smell—of a working inner-city farm that was only metres away from residential towers and townhouses?

For the action group, there were a range of other fears and concerns that coalesced under the concept of the privatisation of public space. And when thinking about examples and precedents, the group didn't have to look far. More than one member feared that the convent would become 'another Willsmere'.

• • •

One of the largest psychiatric hospitals ever built in Australia, the Kew Lunatic Asylum—later known as Willsmere—was founded in the nineteenth century. An 1857 report by GW Vivian of the Public Works Office recommended that the asylum be built on a hilltop site near the Yarra River between Princess Street and Yarra Boulevard in Kew. Vivian described the site as:

> a section of land, about 400 acres [162 hectares] in extent, situated on the River Yarra, about 4 miles [6.5 kilometres] from Melbourne, and ½ a mile to the north of the village of Kew … the site selected is a fine slope, elevated about 100 feet [30.5 metres] above the level of the river, admitting of proper drainage and admirably adapted for ornamental grounds, the aspect chosen is south-east, and during the summer months the refreshing influence of the sea-breeze will be felt, without being exposed to south-west gales.

Construction of the asylum's buildings—in an expensive Italianate 'high Victorian' style—began in 1864 and was largely concluded in 1872. The main building, with its French-style mansard roofs, was later described as 'a wedding-cake beauty', and that is a true description. The asylum operated for more than a century, from 1871 until December 1988. In March 1978 it was placed on the Register of the National Estate due to its cultural and historical significance. A principal aspect of the main building's architectural significance was its long facade, reportedly the longest of its type in the Southern Hemisphere.

In 1988, an 'extensive conservation analysis' recommended that most of the original buildings be conserved. Around the same time, and despite community opposition, the Victorian government sold the main building and grounds for conversion into condominium-style residential properties. Property developer Central Equity Ltd turned the complex into a residential development, and Premier Jeff Kennett officially opened it on 27 October 1993.

A condition of the development permit had been that some of the site's heritage be retained and put on display. As a result, Willsmere now features an 'interpretive display' in one of the old wards. On view are documents and the few remaining artefacts left behind by the developer, including architectural fragments, a wheelchair and an electroshock machine. The Australian Science Archives Project (ASAP) at the University of Melbourne created the display, taking on the project 'despite the minimal funding because supposedly we were the only people who could and would undertake a project like this'. According to ASAP, the 'conservation architect' on the redevelopment project had tried to preserve aspects of the original buildings but in reality 'almost every trace of the building's past [was] eradicated'. Among the few traces that survived were window scratches made by inmates of the Female Paying Patients Ward.

Press coverage of a 2016 'open house' at Willsmere claimed that some of the tower penthouses were selling for up to $2 million each. Jack Lord, chair of the Willsmere Owners Corporation, conceded to a journalist that in the past the residents had not fulfilled their responsibility to share the site's heritage with the public, but that this would change.

It's natural that members of the St Heliers Action Group would think of the Kew Asylum redevelopment: there were profound resonances between Willsmere and Abbotsford. Buildings on the two sites dated from around the same period. They were built on the same stretch of the Yarra River. Both were major social institutions in their day, and both were of enduring architectural and heritage importance. Australand's vision would see the convent undergo Willsmere-style redevelopment. Marketing puff called Willsmere a 'fully gated residential complex' offering 'tranquil, serene and friendly living at its best'—not what the action group wanted for the convent.

Lewis was experienced in the architectural field of 'adaptive re-use'. A resident of Kew, he knew the history of Willsmere well and had witnessed and lamented the failed efforts to save it. He and the other action group members were intent on avoiding a repeat of that loss. They would do what they could to preserve the convent's heritage value. That value had multiple facets. Lee and Lewis brought to the project the concept of 'heritage in use'. There was no point, they thought, in just preserving the buildings as artefacts frozen in time: the site needed to be used.

Apart from the convent site's formal heritage significance, there was a less formal and more verbal heritage that adhered to the buildings and the riverside grounds. Over hundreds of years, the site had accumulated a rich corpus of stories and myths and lore—facts and happenings only half seen and changed in the telling, such as the episode from 1849 in which two local doctors met on the Abbotsford peninsula for a duel. Just one shot was fired; it punctured the hat of the opposing doctor and 'creased' his head. The crease wasn't fatal and the dispute ended amicably, with an exchange of handshakes.

Then there was the story from 1884 of two youths—William Holt and Henry Peace—who were brought before the Collingwood Court charged with bathing in the Yarra during prohibited hours: 'They were seen by Constables Chisholm and Hogan in the river, near the Abbotsford Convent, on Wednesday last, about 6 p.m. Mr. Alley said that river bathers were becoming an intolerable nuisance to all respectable people. The defendants were fined forty shillings each.'

On a Friday evening in 1905, another group of boys organised a raid on the convent's orchards that had a tragic ending: 'The gathering of fruit was in full swing when one lad raised a cry of "Yow! The police are coming." Panic seized the boys and there was a general stampede. Afterwards it was found that one of them was missing.'

The fear was that the missing boy had collided with another boy and fallen into the river. A search ensued but he wasn't found. And then, the following day, the worst fears were realised: the boy's body was found under a snagging dredge near Johnston Street, about 800 metres from where he was thought to have entered the water.

There were other accidental drownings, and intentional ones, along with thefts, assaults, vandalism and other crimes. There was also a rich tradition of pranks and strange happenings, including the sketchy modern story of a goat dropped off in the convent meadows in the early hours of the morning after a stint at Richmond Police Station. Other rumours spoke of bacchic midnight dances and sundry dark rituals. At the height of the convent era, locals out 'fishing' would steal the convent's chickens. Birds thus stolen were referred to as 'fish with feathers'.

Most important of all, there were the stories of life inside the convent: the stories of the nuns and penitents and orphans and inmates who lived and died behind the wall.

4
Neither pot nor pan

EIGHTEEN FIFTY-ONE WAS a big year for the people of the Port Phillip District. On 1 July, the district officially became the nucleus of the new colony of Victoria, named in honour of the Queen. (An oak tree planted on Edward Curr's Abbotsford Estate celebrated victory in the 'leave' campaign.) And just a few weeks after the colony officially came into being, gold was discovered at Clunes, north of Ballarat, and at Andersons Creek, north-east of Melbourne. Soon more discoveries would be made, including a world-class alluvial deposit at Ballarat.

Gold sparked a two-pronged mass movement of people. Gold-seekers rushed to Melbourne from the other colonies and from abroad, and residents left the city for the gold-bearing countryside. The number of Melburnians ebbed and flowed, but the population of the colony as a whole exploded from 77,345 people in 1851 to 125,000 by 1857 and 540,322 by 1861. Gold helped Melbourne establish impressive institutions at remarkably early dates: a university (1853), a museum (1854), a free public library (1854), houses of parliament (1855–56), a public art gallery (1861) and zoological gardens (1862).

The city was soon home to grand neighbourhoods but also to impoverished ones, like those of Carlton, Collingwood, East Melbourne and North Melbourne. In central Melbourne, Bourke Street, Stephen Street and Little Lonsdale Street ('Little Lon') quickly became notorious for gambling and prostitution. Robert Hoddle's lanes became 'poorly lit public urinals, rubbish tips and breeding grounds for criminals'. Destitute men and women lived in temporary shelters on the banks of the Yarra and a bleak 'Canvas Town' of tents and huts sprawled across Melbourne's south.

The gold rush had profound effects on Victoria's social fabric. Many of the men who laboured on the goldfields left behind widows and deserted wives in inner Melbourne. Infant mortality spiked in the gold-rush years, as did the number of abandoned and orphaned children. Irish girls, sent to the colony in large numbers to escape the Great Famine, swelled the urban poor. Many of the new arrivals had high hopes of a better life, but in reality the outlook was grim. Jobs were scarce, working conditions poor. Many girls and women turned to prostitution as a way to work on better terms. Historian Catherine Kovesi summarised the awful calculus: 'Even if a woman took only one paying customer a day, at the going rate of two shillings and sixpence for a short time (at the bottom end of the market) she would earn more in a week than as a skilled tailoress.'

The plight of girls and women attracted the attention of religious orders such as the Sisters of Mercy, who resolved in 1858 or thereabouts to establish 'a House of Mercy for the protection of young virtuous women who find themselves unemployed'. Admitting about sixty women each year, the House focused on 'virtuous women [of] good character'. According to Kovesi, the sisters' rule forbade them from working with or sheltering women of 'questionable morals'. Other orders, too, focused on the 'deserving poor'—people in 'legitimate distress' rather than 'fallen women'.

That loaded term, 'fallen women', was applied to a wide range of people: sex workers, 'deviants', 'vagrants', thieves, alcoholics, the mentally ill, women guilty of 'disorderly conduct', and unmarried women with young or unborn children. In early Melbourne, the members of this large constituency were sorely underserviced. In 1857, only two places offered shelter for them: a small, stern, lay Anglican refuge in South Yarra (later in Carlton), and the Female Reformatory Home, founded by the Melbourne City Court Missionary Society. The leader of the Sisters of Mercy, Mother Ursula Frayne, noticed the shortage of support and had a timely idea: could this problem have an international solution?

• • •

Based in Angers, France, the Sisters of the Good Shepherd took an active approach to their work. In addition to vows of poverty, chastity and obedience, the sisters promised to labour for the salvation of souls: 'While they strive after excellence themselves they reach out a hand to those who are sinking beneath the quicksands of what is called life.' By word and example, the Sisters of the Good Shepherd taught:

> that there is no slavery but sin, no freedom but that which Christ has purchased, that no matter what the past may have been, to what depths of degradation a soul may have sunk, how wide the chasm or impassable the gulf which separates the child of misfortune from the home of her youth or the honest field of labour, yet she is welcome in the home the Church provides for her, and if there be in that sin-stained soul a particle of faith, a ray of hope, a spark of charity, then God himself will bend down to bind up the bruised reed and pour a flame of divine love into the smoking flax.

The sisters' order is rich with beginnings. Formally, it was founded in France in 1835 by Mother Mary Euphrasia Pelletier, but the congregation also traced its origins further back, to an order founded by a secular priest of Normandy—the venerable John Eudes—in 1641. That order, known as the Institute of Our Lady of Charity of the Refuge, was all but destroyed during the French Revolution. And the Order of the Good Shepherd has an even earlier origin: the Biblical moment when Mary of Bethany (conflated, in medieval tradition, with Mary Magdalen) anointed the feet of Jesus.

Whatever their origins, the sisters were just what Melbourne needed. Mother Ursula shared her idea with Dr James A Goold, the Bishop of Melbourne. Could steps be taken to establish in Melbourne a branch of the Sisters of the Good Shepherd?

In 1859, Bishop Goold contacted the foundress and superioress of the order, Mother Mary Euphrasia Pelletier. Might she be able to send sisters to Melbourne? Negotiations began for a 'Mission of Australia'. Initially, sufficient funds couldn't be found and the plans had to be shelved, but in 1862, Bishop Goold again made contact with the order, this time via its Limerick branch. Was there another way? Could Irish sisters be sent out to help in Melbourne?

The answer was yes. Mary Euphrasia acted with determination to establish an Irish-Australian foundation. In November 1862, she received the necessary authorisation from Cardinal Patrizi Naro in Rome, and on 10 January 1863, she announced her intentions to the sisters and nominated the four who would establish the antipodean outpost. In February that year, four Irish Sisters of the Good Shepherd embarked for Melbourne aboard the ship *Forest Rights*. Their mission: to establish an Australian branch that would 'bring back to a life of virtue and peace poor straying women who wish to return to the Divine Saviour of souls ere this short life closes, and time for repentance is at an end'.

Mother Mary of St Joseph (Doyle), aged twenty-seven, led the group. Born in Roscrea, Ireland, she had joined the order in Angers in 1858 and completed her novitiate with the specific intention of working as a missionary abroad. Her companions on this mission were Sister Mary of St Thomas Aquinas (formerly Brigid Lalor), aged twenty-five, from Castledermot; Sister Mary of St Francis Xavier (formerly Helen Corbett), aged thirty-two, from Askeaton; and Sister Mary of St Alphonsus (formerly Anastasia Lacey), possibly from Rahan.

The sisters travelled with Father Crane, who'd been chaplain to a community of Dominicans in Dublin but was advised to go to Melbourne for his health. Though the sisters travelled in first-class cabins, the voyage was difficult. The sisters fell ill and the intense heat made things worse, as did the storms interspersed with periods of dead calm. One especially violent storm hit the ship late in the voyage and drove it off course. As a consequence, the journey took almost forty more days than planned.

On 22 June 1863, land was sighted. Two days later—on the feast day of St John the Baptist—the ship cast anchor at Sandridge. Bishop Goold sent two clergymen to meet the sisters on board the *Forest Rights*: Dr John Bleasdale and Father W Reardon. Mother Ursula Frayne and her assistant, Mother Anne Xavier Dillon, met the sisters at Queen's Dock and took them to the House of the Sisters of Mercy in Fitzroy. Bishop Goold was soon there to welcome them, too, and to give them letters from Angers.

The uniform of the Sisters of Mercy was a traditional and somewhat sombre habit. The contrast with the 'French nuns'—as the sisters were popularly called—was striking. Each of the new arrivals wore a black veil, a robe of cream serge, a broad scapular of the same material, a blue woollen girdle, shoes of undressed leather, 'guimpe' and 'bandeaux' of unstarched linen, a large 'chaplet' of white bone beads, cross from cincture, and a large silver heart suspended from the neck.

The foreign sisters were exotic and intriguing, but Bishop Goold soon made a difficult confession: he had neither land nor money for them. He did, however, offer to lend them his carriage. With Frayne, the sisters began to search Melbourne for a suitable place to establish their foundation. The specifications for the site were clear: there had to be room for penitent girls and women, a section for the Sisters Magdalen, a section for the Sisters of the Good Shepherd themselves, and sections for each of the other apostolates. Spacious grounds would provide peace and quiet, and enable the convent to be self-sufficient.

Mary Euphrasia was adamant. If a suitable place couldn't be found, then the foundation shouldn't go ahead: 'Never found a house for our Magdalens if you haven't a suitable property. They need fresh air and solitude. You will only expose them to dangers and temptations if you put them where there is no garden and adequate accommodations, where they cannot be quite separate from the other categories.'

After a few days of searching, the sisters were shown a large, unoccupied house that sat among 6 acres (2.4 hectares) of orchards, vineyards and gardens on the Yarra River. The house that John Orr had built. Abbotsford House. In their report back to Angers, the sisters recorded their immediate response on seeing the property: a cry of

'Here it is!' The younger nuns in particular were won over. Mother Mary of St Joseph described the house with rapturous words:

> large and handsome with fine lofty rooms and verandah all round, and a tempting garden by the Yarra's bank, with fine fruit trees, peaches, pears, apricots, apples, lemons, grapes and mulberry trees, under which were violets growing so profusely that the air was scented with them.

The sisters purchased the house and grounds for £3500, a very considerable sum in 1863. Bishop Goold did have some money after all: he contributed £1000 on condition that he could later build a church on the site. On 22 July, the feast day of St Mary Magdalen, the bishop and the sisters celebrated the purchase with a mass. To host this event the sisters selected and decorated the best room of their new house; that room would serve for several years as their chapel. On the occasion of the first mass, there were only six chairs in the whole establishment for the use of the nuns and their visitors, so as soon as the mass had been celebrated, the party moved to the House of Mercy for a proper sit-down breakfast.

Over the following days, the Sisters of the Good Shepherd and the Sisters of Mercy laboured side by side to prepare Abbotsford's spaces for living and working. The nuns worked hard but in a jubilant spirit: 'There was a magic in the answering smiles that flashed from face to face when eye met eye—a magic in the sympathetic atmosphere which made labour a thing of joy.'

On 19 August, the sisters moved in. And less than a week later, the convent officially opened. The sisters and Bishop Goold invited prominent Catholics from across Melbourne and the bishop again celebrated a mass. The Sisters of Mercy donated £20; other attendees gave a combined £81. Edward Curr's son, Edward Micklethwaite Curr, and his wife, Margaret, paid for the convent's first crucifix and candlesticks. Michael Curtain of East Melbourne gave the sisters a cow. Mrs Devaney of Collingwood gave a churn and other dairy essentials. Michael O'Grady was another early donor.

A day or two later, Curtain called on the sisters and discovered that their new cow was 'being milked into a small jug, for want of a pail!' 'Dismissing "Eliza", the would be dairymaid, for the time, he sent for a pail, knelt, and milked the cow himself—an object-lesson greatly appreciated by "the maiden all forlorn".'

In 1863, the future Bishop of Ballarat had been one of the first to meet the nuns when they came to Melbourne. In 1900 he told a different version of the story of the convent's first cow. 'There was a little farm here for them,' he said, 'and I thought that we might stock it for them. So seven of us arranged to give a cow apiece. Well, six others gave their cows, but mine was a bit late in arriving, and, lo and behold ye, the day after my cow arrived the other six cows were dead.'

(In 1916 there would be another farmyard incident. *The Advocate* reported it as follows: 'On the eve of the Good Shepherd's feast, celebrated on the second Sunday after Easter, the Great Office was sung by the nuns, according to the custom of their Order. During the day a stray sheep (that had escaped from a large flock in passing) swam across the river right into the convent grounds, and was caught by the gardener, who said that he considered the occurrence "the luckiest of omens"!—adding that if no owner turned up, the "lost sheep" should decidedly be kept "within the fold." The animal was conducted to the farmyard.')

In the first days of the convent there were other teething problems, too:

> when Father England sent the first bag of coal for the kitchen, the good priest caused much hilarity afterwards in informing friends how he thus discovered that the poor nuns had neither pot nor pan! Long years afterwards old benefactors were heard to boast proudly: 'Sure, didn't I know "Abbotsford" when it hadn't even a pan, woman dear?'

Abbotsford's location was important. Apart from the attractions of the riverside environs, it was close to some of the most disadvantaged and densely populated parts of Melbourne. Though the site was close to Hoddle's grid, it was still strikingly rural. The local council offered a bounty of two shillings and sixpence for snakes killed in the area; the bounty was paid frequently. (In the 1860s the snakes were so bold they even menaced people in Collins Street.)

Snakes weren't the only wildlife to cause problems for the sisters. Abbotsford House had stood untenanted for a long time, as they reported to Angers:

> Now you can imagine, dear sisters, a vast house empty for three years, in which spiders have gracefully draped their webs from corner to corner of the rooms, using all their skill in forming draperies in every design worked in the most elegant, most fantastic crochet. The windows were used as entry points for possums, kangaroos and rock-wallabies. The corridors, verandahs, kitchen were decorated with the nests of birds large and small, while lizards and mice paraded across the floor, accompanied by a troop of insects. We will always remember our first evening in our new monastery and our fright during meditation time. At this moment kangaroos, wild cats, possums, hoot-owls, owls, bats commenced their games; we trembled to hear their thumping, we thought we were surrounded by ghosts.

The 'mournful and eerie cries' were just one cause of the sisters' uneasy nights:

> There was no light save that lent by candles—a dim, ghostly radiance in which the younger Sisters' eyes looked like those of scared children who have just laid down a book wherein hobgoblins played their thrilling part. And added to this was, the fact, soon ascertained, that most of the doors were minus locks: no matter for joking over in those days of early Melbourne, when one was far from police protection and when one knew not what sort of folk might be wandering about. Drink was then the curse of the city, and, worst of all, a 'fashionable curse'.

'Native cats'—probably quolls—'roamed at liberty under floors and on roof and ceiling':

> The unearthly noises those creatures made led the Sisters to fancy that they were animals the size of tigers, till, summoning up their courage and investigating for themselves, they saw them peeping from under the verandah with their piercingly bright eyes. One wild look at the Sisters, then a general scamper through the place in the fast-falling darkness.

Birds, koalas and possums also disturbed the sisters' rest. Fortunately the human welcome was much more pleasing. People from across Melbourne and even further afield greeted the sisters' arrival in the colony with interest and gratitude. On 9 September 1863, the *Geelong Advertiser* reported:

> The premises known as Abbotsford house, the grounds of which so beautifully extend to the Yarra facing Studley park, have now become the property of the 'Sisters of the Good Shepherd', who state that their chief object in incurring such a liability is to 'found near Melbourne a house of their institute, with a view to bring back to a life of virtue and peace poor straying women who wish to return to the Divine Saviour of souls ere this short life closes, and time for repentance is at an end.' It is intended to make the institution self-supporting for the future; a debt, however, has yet to be wiped off, and a bazaar is to be held to assist in discharging the same early in November next.

On 26 September, the first penitent arrived at the convent: Anne Kelly, aged seventeen, was given a new name, 'Marie'. She was soon joined by other girls and women, and by the end of the year, six penitents (one of whom soon left) had been received into the newly named Magdalen Asylum. As the sisters reported to their benefactors and friends, the women were in grave need of help:

> With very few exceptions the unfortunate, penitent women, when they apply at the convent gate for admittance, are in a state of

> destitution and rags, weakened by disease, by drink, and a long course of utter desperation, and consequently not only unfit to earn anything for a long time, but needing to be clothed afresh from head to foot, and very frequently to be placed under careful medical treatment. And even when restored to health, it is only after a lapse of a considerable time that they are brought round to the homely occupation in which they are to be employed.

Apart from penitents, the sisters welcomed aspiring nuns. On 11 November, Ellen Fennessy was received as a novice sister and was given, on Mary Euphrasia's express instruction, the name in religion of St Euphrasie: 'Sister Mary of St Euphrasie Fennessy became thereby the first Australian woman to enter the order and was to become instrumental in the expansion of the order in the southern hemisphere.'

5
A positive alternative

UNDER THE FORMAL planning process, submissions relating to Australand's redevelopment and the associated planning amendment had to be received by Yarra Council no later than 24 December 1997.

Two-and-a-half weeks before Christmas, Melbourne was winding down. Schools were breaking up. Offices were holding end-of-year parties. People were tying off loose ends before the holiday season. It was in this environment that word of the proposed development and amendment spread even further, and the campaign swung into action.

Members of the action group immediately made contact with the public authorities and heritage institutions that would have an interest in the site and the campaign and understood what was at stake. The members wrote letters and made phone calls. They sought advice from the National Trust, the departments of heritage, arts, parks and infrastructure, and other organisations and people who might advise or join or endorse the campaign, and whose responsibilities might overlap in a useful way.

The action group members also drew on their personal networks, enlisting friends and family members and other people from all parts of Melbourne and beyond. On the ground at Abbotsford they introduced themselves to people visiting the Children's Farm or riding bikes on the trail or enjoying the nearby parks. They contacted residents further afield, including across the river in Kew. Please, the campaign urged, submit your objections before Christmas.

At the same time, the campaigners took their first formal step in the planning process. The action group requested that Yarra Council hold more public briefings with more transparent and extensive communication, and adopt a broader process involving all Yarra councillors. Further, the group sought an extension of the formal public exhibition period and the deadline for acceptance of submissions, and deferral of any decision on Amendment L54.

That amendment was wide in its scope and audacious in its goals. It sought to change the conditions for development on the convent site and remove the rights of residents to object or to be informed of any changes. It included rezoning of the land to residential; removal of the Skyline Area Control, modification of the River Concept Plan, and an exemption from the Floodway Management Plan. Hilary Rankin expressed a fear that the whole action group shared: passing the amendment would mean 'open slather' for developers. It just had to be stopped.

Yarra Council held a Christmas function at the Edinburgh Gardens in North Fitzroy. John Phillips was a councillor who would soon begin a term as mayor, and Jo Kinross politely buttonholed him about the convent site. 'It's all well and good to protest,' Phillips replied, 'but what would be there instead?'

Most of the concerned residents had had the same thought. Saying no wasn't enough: they would certainly fail if they took a purely oppositional stance. The action group needed a positive alternative to take forward. 'Not only do we have to stop the redevelopment,' Kinross said, 'but we need an alternative for the site.'

At the next action group meeting, everyone agreed that the campaign had to be constructive. Their job wasn't just to block the amendment and the development proposal: they had to put forward their own viable proposal. But what should that alternative look like? What could and should the site become?

• • •

Little did the action group members know that the site had a long history of people's colourful dreams for it. In the 1860s, for example, Samuel Moss had made grand plans for Abbotsford House that were all about pleasure. There would be a 'pleasure hall' (something like a club or a casino) and a cafe; pleasure boats would ply between it and central Melbourne; and the visitors would enjoy all manner of entertainments.

Moss lacked the resources to match his grandiose plans. 'Abbotsford' would never become a 'palace of pleasure'. Other ideas, however, would be put forward. In 1922, moves were made to shift Melbourne's beloved zoo to Studley Park and the nearby riverside environs. The zoo move was canned, but an even more drastic proposal was put forward in 1933. At a local council meeting, Mr E Allen of Ringwood suggested that the Yarra River should be diverted at Abbotsford 'to enable the present bed to be searched for gold':

> Mr Allen suggested that a cut should be made from the boat sheds above Dight's Falls to the convent, straightening the river, giving a boat route from the Bay to Heidelberg, and obviating a large expenditure in renewing Johnston Street bridge. The site of the bridge should be filled with spoil from the cut, he suggested, and the present bed gradually reclaimed. The fine gold in the present bed would meet the cost, Mr Allen suggested. The suggestion was referred to a committee.

In the 1970s, consideration was given to demolishing all the buildings on the site, thereby turning it into a blank slate for comprehensive redevelopment. In 1986, the convent site was put forward as a possible permanent home for Australia's national circus company, Circus Oz. Another idea from the 1980s was to turn the site into a private university; this progressed to such an extent that the project's proponents publicly named Sir Ninian Stephen as the future university's inaugural chancellor. But that proposal, too, came to naught.

When the St Heliers Convent Action Group turned its thinking to site-use options, a generous range of artistic, social, industrial and commercial alternatives presented themselves. The site could become a school, a wellness centre, a boatbuilding workshop, a theatre venue, a business incubator, a centre for Indigenous culture, or any of a wide range of different types of museum.

Among the many concepts that were floated, a few stood out. One frontrunning idea was to make the best use of a happy coincidence in the geography of art in Melbourne. Two major art institutions were already on the Yarra River: the National Gallery of Victoria, just south of the city; and Heide, on the river at Heidelberg. Could Abbotsford become a centre for art conservation and display that strengthened this riparian nexus? Could the Yarra, in other words, become not only a 'river of mists' but a 'valley of the arts'?

Kinross and Nigel Lewis took a purposeful walk around the convent site, looking at the buildings and grounds through a prospective lens and imagining how the assets might best be re-used with minimal intervention. Art and culture? Definitely. Education? Yes, that made sense, too—there was, after all, a long history of teaching and training on the site. At the end of their walk, Kinross and Lewis had the shared thought that an 'arts and education precinct' would be a viable option.

What Kinross saw in her mind's eye at this time was remarkably specific and concrete. Artist studios inside the heritage spaces. Community markets outside. Wellness services. Educators. A diverse range of people busily using the site for an equally eclectic set of purposes. She would keep that picture in view throughout the campaign.

A later variant of the 'arts precinct' idea saw the convent hosting an 'arts hotel' that accommodated visiting artists. Under yet another variant, Lewis and his partner drew up plans for a four-storey apartment building on the northern car park, with the estimated development proceeds of around $7 million to be used to 'save' the convent by funding the restoration and conservation of the heritage buildings and grounds. Like many options that were considered, this compromise solution ultimately turned out to be unviable; the campaigners' consideration of it would have unexpected implications down the track.

In considering the various options and proposals, the action group would arrive at a clearer picture of what the site might become, and what the campaigners would be prepared to get behind. The solution for the site had to be community owned and driven. It had to preserve the site's heritage and integrity. Public access had to be maintained—that was paramount. And the site had to be able to stand on its own two feet. The activities ultimately selected had to be intrinsically viable and sustainable but not flagrantly commercial; an overly commercial solution would just be Australand in another guise. Residential development was out of the question because it would restrict public access and because it, too, could lead to redevelopment by another route. The campaigners were reluctant to countenance even a small proportion of residential use, as that could be the thin end of a residential wedge.

With these parameters in mind, the campaign team gave more and more solidity to their vision. They would soon form an 'ideas' subcommittee to consider alternative uses for the site. (Other subgroups formed around this time were Publicity, Media Liaison, Submissions, Administration, Coordination of Volunteers, and Fundraising/Events.) The ideas subcommittee and the campaign as a whole would have to walk a tightrope between economic failure and excessive commerciality. The new vision for the site had to succeed, but it had to do so in the right way.

• • •

Just two days before the Christmas Eve deadline, the campaign to save the convent had a small victory. The City of Yarra agreed to extend to 22 February 1998 the formal public exhibition period and the due date for submissions. The council also agreed to hold a more comprehensive public briefing—one that all Yarra councillors would attend. The victory might have been modest but the campaigners were delighted. Theirs would be a particularly happy holiday season.

Early in the new year, the action group ramped up the campaign. They joined forces with nearby sympathetic bodies such as the Studley Park Association and the Friends of Yarra Bend Park. They encouraged people concerned about the future of the convent to write to Heritage Victoria and the Department of Infrastructure, as well as to Yarra Council, and to attend the upcoming 22 February public briefing and any other planned meetings concerning the convent site, whether convened by the council, the developers or the objectors to the development. They lobbied councillors and other locals, and present and former politicians who lived outside the area.

Though strongly progressive in spirit and flavour, the action group agreed that the campaign mustn't be party-political. Being bound to one party would be a tactical blunder as it would limit options and create a powerful set of opponents. The members cultivated political support from all parties, thereby laying a foundation for the campaign to receive public support from the Australian Labor Party, the Greens and the Democrats as well as from individuals in the governing Liberal Party.

The group also made another smart move. In February 1998, the St Heliers Convent Action Group became the Abbotsford Convent Coalition (ACC). This was astute branding. The new name would better distinguish the campaign from Australand's 'St Heliers' development, would anchor the contest in a specific geography, and would highlight both a fact and an aspiration: the fact that the community owned the campaign, and the aspiration that the community could own the site. The word 'coalition' was important, too, and deliberate. Alternatives such as 'cooperative' sounded too political. And 'coalition' nicely captured the campaign's ethos of openness and its spirit of working together.

Another early decision was that the campaigners would form a corporation. Incorporation of the ACC would give solidity and formality to the group and its mission, afford the members some legal protection if the fight got really nasty, and help in their efforts to raise money and gather resources for the campaign. The incorporated ACC would formally pursue three specific goals: to ensure the former convent site was protected and accessible; to preserve the site in community ownership; and to protect the neighbouring Collingwood Children's Farm.

6
Growth

NOT LONG AFTER the sisters first moved into Abbotsford House, the building was already feeling crowded. Different rooms had to serve multiple purposes. At night, for example, the sewing classroom had to be used as a dormitory. A question confronted Mother Mary of St Joseph (Doyle): how might the sisters buy 'St Helier's', the property next door?

A decade earlier, Edward Curr's widow, Elizabeth, had advertised St Helier's for sale. Along with a spacious five-bedroom mansion, the 16-acre (6.5-hectare) estate included an established garden, a six-stall stable and dairy, and thriving orchards, vineyards and paddocks. Despite these attractions, no buyer was found. Elizabeth's daughter, Agnes, and her son-in-law, Hastings Cunningham, moved in.

Now, the Currs seemed to have no intention of selling St Helier's. Mother Mary of St Joseph sought special help. Near the fence that divided the two properties, she placed a small statue of her namesake, St Joseph, 'imploring his aid that the suitable land on the other side might yet become a permanent property for the "children" of her anxious solicitude'. Somehow, this tactic worked. In September 1865, Elizabeth agreed to sell St Helier's to the sisters for £4000.

Of the sixteen acres, six were under cultivation. The sisters expressed the intention of using St Helier's for the Magdalen Asylum, 'so that they could separate completely the penitents from the reformatory children'. Behind this intention was a nineteenth-century idea of social 'contamination'—the concept that social ills could pass from one group to another through contact. The sisters erected fences to enclose the newly expanded convent and asylum. This was the prelude to an ambitious program of building within the convent grounds.

In 1867, Melbourne's *Illustrated Australian News for Home Readers* reported an important event:

> The first stone of a new building in connection with the Magdalen Asylum and Juvenile Reformatory at Abbotsford, conducted by the Nuns of the Good Shepherd, was laid on 3rd inst., by the Very Rev. Dr. Fitzpatrick, V.G., in the presence of about 2000 persons … The nuns have three classes of inmates under their control, namely, penitent females who have been rescued from the profession of sin, criminal female children who are sent to the reformatory by the magistrates, and little ones whose parents are unable wholly to support them, but may be in a position to contribute a small sum periodically towards their maintenance in this establishment. The new building about to be erected is intended to afford additional accommodation to the juvenile inmates, whose quarters are at present inconveniently overcrowded, and to afford an opportunity of receiving more of these applicants who daily have to be refused admission for want of sufficient room.

The following year, on the Feast of St Joseph, the order officially opened the large and commodious two-storey building that would house the new industrial and reformatory schools. More than 150 friends and patrons attended the opening. As the *Illustrated Australian News for Home Readers* reported in June 1868, the convent now consisted of three main buildings: the Magdalen Asylum for 'penitent females', the Industrial School for 'fatherless and neglected and criminal children', and the nuns' own residence. The sisters resided in Abbotsford House, the Magdalens in St Helier's. The new building, for 'the juvenile portion of the inmates',

> is a fine brick building, which at a distance looks like a factory or a mill. The establishment stands on the north bank of the Yarra, the

> spacious and well-cared grounds extending down to the margin of the river … Studley Park in the background lends an attractive air to the scenery of the locality. At a short distance above the asylum the river is crossed by a substantial wooden bridge of recent date.

On 13 June 1869, Mother Mary of St Joseph (Doyle), foundress and prioress of the convent, died. She was the fourth Sister of the Good Shepherd to pass away in the colony. The deceased sisters were interred within the convent grounds. The bishop and the Catholic community raised funds, and the order engaged architect TA Kelly to design a mortuary chapel that would honour the legacy of Mother Mary of St Joseph and the other recently deceased nuns.

The plans were soon expanded. Instead of a mortuary chapel, the convent would have a church: the Church of the Immaculate Conception. Kelly produced a cruciform plan with the octagonal chancel at the northern end. Modelled in part on the mother church at Angers, the design called for three types of stone: bluestone for the superstructure, Malmsbury stone for the strings and bases and copings, and Spring Bay freestone to dress the doors and windows.

In 1870, the Very Rev. Dean Fitzpatrick laid the foundation stone for the new church within the convent enclosure. The following year, the church opened in a partially completed form—there wasn't enough money to finish it. The eastern transept, intended for the accommodation of the penitents, was completed first. Of the western transept, intended for the use of the public, only a small portion had been built. The nave, intended for the use of the sisters, was also unfinished. *The Advocate* nevertheless applauded the elegance of the new structure:

> [The chancel] is lighted by two light traceried windows at either side, and a small wheel or rose window in the centre. The latter is beautifully glazed in stained glass, the subjects represented being in the centre the Lamb, while the emblems of the Passion are ranged in the surrounding circles. This window has been executed by Messrs. Fergusson and Urie of this city, and has been, we understand, presented to the Nuns of the Good Shepherd by the architect of the church … A covered porch gives access to

> the ground floor, and a circular turret staircase to the upper. This turret is carried up by a spire, octagonal in form, to a … height of 50 feet [15 metres], terminating in a carved finial, the spire being ornamented by bands, open-pierced work, and gablets. The centre of the gable is pierced by a large wheel window of elegant design most chastely carved.

The Advocate speculated that the unfinished building had cost 'not much under £4000'.

Five-and-a-half years after the laying of the foundation stone of the convent's first church, Archbishop Goold laid the cornerstone for a major extension. As *The Age* reported,

> The portion of the existing place of worship allotted to visitors and occasional attendants having been found far too small a space for the rapidly increasing number of worshippers … the Sisters of the convent have, at an estimated cost of £1700, recently initiated a plan of extension at the northern transept, the building being carried 28 feet [8.5 metres] further in this direction by a width of 25 feet. Mr. T. A. Kelly, the architect, has designed a pretty little structure, which, in point of style, will of course be in accord with the existing edifice. A handsome window filled with geometric tracery will be one of the principal features in the new gable, and the stairs giving access to the gallery will be constructed in an octagonal turret terminating in a spire surmounted by a carved finial, at a total elevation of about fifty feet.

In 1880, an 'interesting ceremony' took place at the convent:

> The large bell, which in a few days will be suspended in the tower of the convent church, was solemnly blessed by his Grace the Archbishop, assisted by Rev. Dean Donaghy and Rev. T. Cahill, S. J. The deep, solemn and musical tones of this massive bell will soon be familiar to the ears, not only of the religious community resident within the convent, but likewise to those of the faithful

> who dwell around the convent within a radius of some miles. Thrice each day its sound will remind them of the visit of the archangel to the Virgin of Nazareth, and will invite them to unite with the religious in offering a tribute of praise and thanksgiving to her and to Him who through her vouchsafed to become our Saviour.

Two final phases of construction would complete the church. The first of these concluded in 1890:

> When the late Superioress of the Abbotsford Convent (Sister Mary J. Curtain) died, a number of ladies belonging, not only to the Roman Catholic Church, but to all branches of the Christian community who know her worth, subscribed to a fund for the purpose of erecting a lasting memorial in recognition of her many good works. A substantial sum of money was subscribed, and the memorial has taken the form of adding a spire to the tower of the convent, which has been recently completed by Messrs Tappin Gilbert & Dennehy, the architects. A portion of the old tower was taken down to enable a new belfry to be constructed, and the spire now reaches a height of 100ft [30.5 metres] from the ground. Its architectural character is Gothic, in harmony with the whole building. It is finished at the top with a bold carved finial, on which stands a fine wrought iron cross picked out with gold … A splendid gift of a new clock for the tower … has been made by Mr Thomas Gaunt, the well-known clock and watch maker of Bourke street, and it is now in working order.

Then, in 1897, the Penitents' Transept of the Church of the Immaculate Conception was completed, and charitable subscribers funded a 'Memorial Crown' for the Statue of the Blessed Virgin. The crown, crafted from Australian gold and ornamented with jewels by Messrs Gaunt & Co. of Melbourne, was used for the first time on 8 December, for the Feast of the Immaculate Conception. The following year, the interior of the church was renovated and redecorated. Fresco paintings were installed and the walls and ceiling coloured.

The completed Church of the Immaculate Conception is notable for its Memorial Crown and frescoes, its clock, and the partitioning of the church's interior to accommodate the different categories of girls and women, enabling them to attend the same services without interacting with each other.

7
A social enterprise

As soon as the concerned Abbotsford residents decided to pursue a positive, viable alternative to residential development of the former convent site, their campaign underwent a radical phase-shift. Not only did the action group and then the Abbotsford Convent Coalition have to put forward the right kind of solution, but they also had to own it, and drive it. Once they were organised and activated, the residents morphed from a 'community interest group' into a 'social enterprise'. This was a difficult transition—one that very few community organisations had managed to pull off.

The transformation from grassroots activists to social entrepreneurs had big implications. Formulating and implementing a large-scale site plan would require specialist expertise and significant resources. And it would draw the residents into a battle that few of them might have anticipated when they first met around Sue Bannerman's kitchen table.

On paper at least, the battle was extremely one-sided. 'It was a David and Goliath struggle,' Charlotte Allen said. 'We had to use every strategy we could.'

'Goliath' was a big corporation with a big profile and deep pockets, backed by investors and governments in Australia and Singapore. 'David' was a group of concerned local residents who had never worked together before, and who had minimal funds and little experience in running a large-scale community campaign, let alone steering a large-scale community development project. Australand was proposing to spend more than $100 million on the project. The residents for their part had little idea of what they were likely to need, and how they might get it.

The campaign kicked off in an era of big money and rampant change in Melbourne. In addition to the private developer, the Abbotsford Convent Coalition was taking on the council, the state premier, the state planning minister, the Urban Land Corporation and other arms of the government—most of which were avowedly pro-development. The political climate in Victoria was particularly fractious and polarised. Though Premier Jeff Kennett could claim many economic achievements, he was proudly hostile to numerous social and public institutions. On a personal level, he and Planning Minister Rob Maclellan played the game of politics in a manner and style that was unapologetically hard and sometimes bruising.

In this environment, the planning process seemed designed to favour the developer and make opposition extremely difficult. Many of the campaigners never imagined that the process would be so gruelling. They found themselves in a war of attrition that was seemingly intended to wear down and dispirit any community voices opposed to a private project. When they looked at previous campaigns, they noticed how many community action groups had been worn down or had simply fallen apart.

At times, the Abbotsford Convent Coalition's efforts to combine community activism and large-scale development felt like trying to mix oil and water. But the campaigners didn't fall apart or fade away. They would quickly get used to the 'two steps forward, one step back' dynamics of the planning system. Organised and agile, they set up the Abbotsford Convent Project Working Group as a rapid-response team of core ACC members plus architects, lawyers, surveyors, financial advisers, building works assessors and project managers who would give their time on a pro bono or 'low bono' basis. Structured and supported in this way, the ACC was a legitimate player performing a legitimate, formal, legal role in an official planning process.

There would soon be more 'bonos'. In April 1998, the De Bono Institute donated an evening session that exposed twelve ACC members to the rigours and benefits of 'parallel thinking'. The success or failure of the Abbotsford campaign would depend on how well the ACC could source and integrate different types of expertise, and how well it could maintain its dual existence as community group and community entrepreneur. For the push to save the convent, aptitude in 'parallel thinking' would be surprisingly important.

Apart from the convent's conventional heritage values and community values, there were mysterious and subjective values, even spiritual ones. Jo Kinross and Sue Bannerman were active in mainstream fields such as counselling and psychology and kinesiology, but also in alternative ones, such as reiki, geomancy and shamanistic healing. Tools from those fields allowed Kinross and Bannerman to bring a spiritual, whole-person awareness to their professional work. When they helped people, they were alert to subjective forces and energies as well as traditional ideas of health and wellbeing.

Other members of the ACC—along with Greg Milne at the Children's Farm—were also in tune with the less visible sides of the universe. At the convent, they detected lines of energy—something like the ancient ley lines of Great Britain. They noticed how the main buildings were deliberately situated in mathematical alignment with other local Catholic landmarks, such as St Ignatius in Richmond and St Joseph's in Northcote. They were alert to coincidences and omens. And they felt in a genuine way the deep magic of the place.

Kinross and Bannerman approached the convent just as they would a person, testing for the colour and intensity and polarity of its energy, and searching for its centre. On one particularly important walk at the site, they searched for the convent's heart—and found it, near a peppercorn tree just inside the St Heliers entrance.

'The site is a very special place,' Kinross said afterwards. 'It has a real energy. And despite the convent's past and the difficult things that happened there, I always felt the energy was positive.'

8
A noble cause

FOR MORE THAN a decade, the Abbotsford Convent had been lit entirely by candles. In 1876, the sisters and their wards were delighted when gas lighting was installed. The installation involved a high degree of 'self-help':

> The late Mr O'Keefe of Abbotsford, upon his death, bequeathed to the Sisters of the Good Shepherd a patent for making gas, and now in the vicinity of the laundry stand the gas works and gasometer in full operation. The convent and all the other buildings are now lighted up with home-made gas, and curiously enough the principal manufacturer is one of the penitent Magdalens.

Over the next two years, the convent's busy building program included a weatherboard hospital and 'Sacred Heart', a permanent building to house the Magdalens. For the latter structure, TA Kelly was again the architect. Richmond's *South Bourke and Mornington Journal* reported in June 1877 on the building works:

> There is now being erected at the eastern end of the convent grounds, two splendid brick buildings from the plans of Mr Kelly and under the superintendence of Mr Henly, the contractor. The boundaries of the buildings are 355 feet [108 metres] all round. Each structure is 25 feet [7.6 metres] wide, and 27 feet high to the

> tie beams, having three large dormitories and two small, refectory, work-room, &c. There are three large rooms 86 [26 metres] by 25½ feet [7.8 metres], and 50 small ones. One third of the building—one side of the courtyard, is to be three storeys high. The bottom storey will consist of a mangling room, dormitories for two of the 'Good Sisters,' a room for imbeciles and invalids, baths, closets, &c. All the buildings are entered by two doors with granite porches and staircases. The buildings are of the Gothic order and when complete will cost £8,000. The walls are constructed of bricks, cement with large footings and rubble foundations brought from Merri Creek. There were only fourteen men engaged at work on Wednesday, but there were to be a number of hands—slaters—employed on Thursday. The buildings will not be finished for twelve or thirteen months at least.

In April 1879, the convent entered a new era with the opening of St Euphrasia's Day School, which would become a local institution in its own right, giving generations of pupils 'all the advantages of a high-class religious and secular training'. By 1888 there would be 221 children enrolled, including twenty-seven boys in the infants class. The practice of segregation was applied to the day school pupils, who were 'as completely cut away from the inmates of the convent as if the school were at the west side of Melbourne'.

The school curriculum included catechism, spelling, arithmetic, English and Australian history, Irish history and roots, home economics, needlework, fancywork and dressmaking. The older children also learned marching, callisthenics and, from 1890, elementary Latin and French. Girls who passed their final sixth-class tests were eligible for a 'Public Service' class that prepared them for the official public service exams.

• • •

With all this building and growth, the land at Abbotsford was beginning to feel crowded. According to the precepts of their order, the sisters needed space for peace and quiet; they were also determined to keep separate the different categories of inmates. The solution was to seek a suitable site elsewhere in Melbourne that could serve as a branch office and sister institution.

In 1880, the Archbishop of Melbourne offered the sisters 55 acres (22 hectares) of land at Oakleigh. The site, on Dandenong Road about 1.5 kilometres from Oakleigh railway station, was suitably rural and isolated. The order decided that the reformatory girls would go there. The girls were wards of the state, sent by the courts to the sisters with explicit terms of 'imprisonment'. *The Argus* reported on the Oakleigh institution:

> This is the only Catholic reformatory in the colony, and the plan adopted by the nuns is to isolate for a time and place under religious treatment the girls placed under their charge, and to train them for farm servants, it being considered better to send them to situations in the country than to the scenes of their former careers. The building will accommodate a hundred, but at present there are only thirty girls to be transferred from Abbotsford.

Work immediately commenced at Oakleigh on a purpose-built complex, which the sisters named 'St James' in honour of the archbishop. At Abbotsford, a weatherboard building was constructed near the farmyard to accommodate the reformatory girls while Oakleigh was under construction. In 1883, after the sisters received formal permission to transfer 'the Government Reformatory for Roman Catholic girls', the move took place.

At the Abbotsford site, building works continued apace. Around 1885, construction began on two structures that would allow the nuns to operate an industrial laundry: Mercator, the main laundry building, and the North Laundry. Up to the years 1964 and 1925 respectively, these two much-used buildings would be altered and added to. In April 1887, construction began on a new building, St Mary's, that would accommodate boarders at St Euphrasia's. Also in that year, 'Providence' was constructed to serve as a 'finishing school' for girls aged from fourteen years who had voluntarily entered the convent and sought to work in service in the community. In 1890 and 1891, various building improvements were carried out and the sisters acquired additional land for their farmyard. In April 1899, building work commenced on a new soap and chaff-cutting department at the Magdalen Asylum. The building program would continue well into the first decade of the twentieth century.

Since their arrival in 1863, the sisters had resided in Abbotsford House. With the expansion of the community's work in Melbourne, that situation was now untenable. In 1900, the order decided to build a proper convent for the sisters, and in May that year, tenders were submitted for the first section of the new convent building. Messrs Christopherson and Brown were chosen as building contractors, and architects Tappin and Smart were selected to design the building that would replace the house that Orr built.

To realise the design, the sisters needed funds. They made plans for a fundraising bazaar whose scale in Melbourne had few precedents. They would call it the 'World's Fair' and hold it in the grand halls of Melbourne's Exhibition Building. On 11 October 1901 the governor-general, Lord Hopetoun, opened the fair. Around 15,000 people attended the opening, the weather beautifully fine and the surrounding gardens in full spring bloom. St Augustine's Band from Geelong played 'God Save the King'. Melbourne's *Argus* reported on the event in appreciative detail:

> The Governor General, who was received with great cheering, thanked the company for the cordial reception which had been extended to him. He was very glad indeed to carry out the duty of declaring the Fair open because the institution which was being helped was one that deserved well of the public, and it had been of the utmost service to the state. The convent was established in 1863, and the buildings alone cost upwards of £80,000 irrespective of the annual charge for upkeep. The object of the bazaar was to provide better accommodation for the devoted women who carried on the work. Considering the good work done by the sisters, and

the fact that for a quarter of a century they had never made any appeal to the public, he had the greatest pleasure in commending the movement to the good offices of the people. (Cheers.) He declared the Fair open.

Archbishop [Thomas] Carr, in moving a vote of thanks to His Excellency and Lady Hopetoun, said that the institution, which provided for the needy of every stage of life, would be benefited by the kindness of their Excellencies in attending to open the bazaar. Their action in this respect was in keeping with the dignity, the impartiality, and the self-sacrifice which they had always displayed since their first arrival in Victoria. (Cheers.) On behalf of the gathering he would extend a welcome to their Excellencies and the gallant soldier who accompanied them. (Loud cheers.)

Mr Duffy, M.L.A., seconded the motion, which was carried with acclamation.

His Excellency, in acknowledging the vote, said that Lady Hopetoun and himself had found in Archbishop Carr a kind, constant, and fervent friend, who had been helpful to them when they had needed help, and therefore they had much pleasure in assisting any movement which the Archbishop wished to aid.

After the speeches the distinguished visitors were taken to the various stalls and sideshows, a duty which they faithfully and good humouredly performed in spite of the inevitable buffeting of a tremendous crowd. They eventually made their way back to the dais, from which they took their departure by the south door.

The arrangements in connection with the opening, which were under the supervision of the hon. secretary, Mr O'Connor, M.L.A., were all that could be desired.

The interior of the Exhibition Building was a marvellous spectacle:

Never before has the Exhibition building looked so fine as at present, with all its cosmopolitan frontages to the main hall, with its handsome entrance gates like the doorways into a castle or abbey, with its garlands of green decked with coloured lights,

> and the imposing lamps which effectively illuminate the whole building. The designers and decorator of the various facades—Messrs M'Crae and Toole and Mr Harry Grist—have turned the building into a kind of foreign city in miniature, a cosmopolis, where a pagoda jostles a Japanese tea house, an Australian bush hut, with its background of stately gums, stands next to an Egyptian temple, while a ruined keep over which floats the Royal Ensign is next to a Chinese dwelling. The idea is to typify by the design of each stall a different country. It would have added a thousand fold to the effect if stall holders had elected to dress in keeping with their various stalls. To see the quaint costumes belonging to each country represented would have been most attractive and charming; while to see the ordinary cotton blouse and skirt as the garb for a seller in an Egyptian temple or a Japanese teahouse is ineffective to say the least of it. So tremendously crowded was the whole building yesterday afternoon that it was impossible to see anything of the wares in the various stalls. Long before 3 o'clock the seats in the body of the hall were all occupied, by half past 3 there was hardly standing room on the ground floor, and the galleries were crowded from end to end, everyone craning forward for the impossible—to hear and see everything that was to be heard and seen. Looking down from the galleries, one saw a packed mass of human beings, the majority being women, though there was a fair sprinkling of the male sex, and there were hundreds of children, many of them tiny infants. Behind the smart fronts of the numerous stalls is certainly gathered an enormous quantity of beautiful things, but it is doubtful if anyone was able to see anything of them during the afternoon. The impression one gained of the huge crowd was of thousands and thousands of gay toques, bonnets and hats forming a kind of sea below, and of a moving crowd endeavouring to see and hear from the balconies.

A great success, the fair ran for several weeks with activities such as running races, bike races and tugs of war. It raised £12,187 net of costs: building work could now safely go ahead.

On 11 November 1900 the foundation stone of the new convent building was laid in the presence of 4000 people. The convent's designated annalist recorded that a further '£3315 was there and then subscribed as a substantial guarantee of goodwill towards the Nuns of the Good Shepherd and their noble cause'. This amount brought the total proceeds of the fundraising campaign to more than £15,000—a triumph for the convent.

The building works proceeded rapidly until, on 17 January 1902, a cross was erected on a section of the new convent's roof. On 13 April, the feast day of the Good Shepherd, Archbishop Carr opened the new central section of the building. Nearly 2000 people witnessed this milestone. In May, the sisters moved into their new home, which was notable for its stained-glass windows, solid wood staircases, long corridors, large reception rooms and windows overlooking the grounds. On some of the doors and window-frames, the faintly grained antipodean timbers were handpainted to simulate the richer European wood grain.

Work soon began on the Western Wing, which would be completed in 1903. Subsequent construction activity ('St Anne's', 1906; the 'South Laundry', aka 'Magdalen Laundry', 1907; and 'Rosina', 1908) would help make the convent one of the largest structures in Melbourne, and the single largest charitable institution in the Southern Hemisphere. According to the Reverend Mother, 'the number of applications received from penitents was greater in 1908 than in any year since the convent was founded'. Designed by William Tappin in the Baroque Revival style, Rosina housed voluntary entrants (mostly older women) who worked alongside the girls in the Magdalen Asylum.

In 1909 *The Advocate* reported:

> Last Sunday afternoon, the Very Rev. Dean Phelan, V.G., blessed the additions recently erected at the Abbotsford Convent for the exclusive use of penitents. These comprise a refectory which will seat 500, a class hall, a recreation-room, dormitories, reception rooms for visitors, and a new oratory, in which Mass was celebrated for the first time on Sunday. The buildings have cost over £8000, but the ceremony of opening them was a private one, and no

> appeal was made to the public for funds ... The construction of the buildings has been carried out under the direction of Mr. Robert Harper, of Abbotsford.

In the same year, the sisters purchased an existing property, 'Home Lodge' on St Heliers Street, for £640.

9
Basket weavers

THE CAMPAIGN TO save the Abbotsford Convent inevitably outgrew the confines of Sue Bannerman's kitchen. The team moved their weekly meetings—sometimes twice-weekly—to a function room at the Retreat Hotel on Nicholson Street, the Boulevard Restaurant in Kew, a little church hall in Abbotsford, and—more often than not—a classroom at the Sophia Mundi Steiner School, also on Nicholson Street. The walls of the classroom were covered with children's artwork and peeling paint. The Abbotsford Convent Coalition members sat in a circle on little chairs, and on cold Melbourne evenings they pulled the chains that activated the wall-mounted radiators.

On 22 January 1998, the City of Yarra held a public meeting to discuss the St Heliers residential proposal and Yarra Planning Scheme Amendment L54. It took place in the Senior Citizens Centre at the rear of Collingwood Town Hall. Hundreds of concerned residents attended; the meeting was standing-room only.

'It was packed,' Charlotte Allen recalled. 'People expressed strong views. They felt locked out of the planning process. Seeing the scale of the community response and the strength of people's views, Australand was horrified!'

For the convent campaigners, the meeting turned out to be highly useful. It provided a platform for them to enlist supporters and to speak against the redevelopment, and gave the campaign a priceless gift: momentum.

Newspapers and television stations soon got wind of the meeting and the campaign. Something interesting, it seemed, was brewing in Abbotsford. In February 1998, Channel 10 broadcast a detailed piece on the site and the contenders, and their competing visions of the convent's future. The Channel 10 crew interviewed ACC members and included their views in the televised piece. After that, the ACC members' telephones began to ring with interview requests from the other television stations, radio stations 3LO, 3AW and 3CR, and newspapers *The Age*, *Herald Sun*, *The Leader* and local papers.

Applying the principles that the campaigners had laid down and building on their initial ideas and personal visions—David Ingamells, for example, envisaged a community-centred precinct that would provide opportunities for young people—the ACC began putting together a proposal for the 'Abbotsford Convent Project'. According to the proposal, the site would become a multipurpose precinct serving objectives relating to the arts, education, tourism, hospitality and community development.

On 25 February, the City of Yarra hosted a second crowded public meeting. Even more people expressed their displeasure with what was afoot. Crucially, the ACC presented its alternative vision for the site. Having heard the community's views and seen the ACC's embryonic proposal, the public meeting adopted two resolutions drafted by the ACC: that Yarra Council abandon Amendment L54; and that it bring together the interested parties to explore viable alternative uses for the site.

All the while, the ACC members kept writing letters and letterboxing. The campaign launched a newsletter and a website. Volunteers set up information tables every weekend on the bike path near the Children's Farm as well as in Studley Park, on Brunswick Street, Fitzroy (opposite the Fitz Cafe), and at shopping centres in Hawthorn and Kew. The ACC used a complex system of volunteer rosters to ensure the tables were always staffed.

Jo Kinross's home became the ACC's de facto office; her kitchen table disappeared under form letters, flyers, faxes and other paperwork. Anna

Lindstad, an architect and ACC member, came up with a striking way to show the scale of the proposed buildings near the bike path: a tethered balloon that rose to the height of the roofline of the proposed tower.

The table volunteers asked people to sign letters of objection to the Australand proposal. Soon there were 10,000 objection letters on their way to Yarra Council, and it was legally bound to reply to every one of them. Faced with this weight of objections, the council put on extra staff to help with the replies, and pleaded with the ACC to stop the flow of letters. Signed pro forma letters were also sent to the local member of the state parliament, until he telephoned Tony Lee and said, 'You've made your point. Now please stop.'

One or two Yarra councillors were active in the 'save' campaign. Some other councillors were sympathetic. But the council as a whole was pro-development. The ACC had so far been able to count on the council for neither practical help nor moral support, but at this point, the council could see the writing on the wall. In March 1998, it abandoned Amendment L54 and agreed to establish a working party. The working party would play multiple critical roles in the battle for the convent, exploring alternative uses of the site, preparing a brief for an architectural design competition and a concept plan for redevelopment of the site, considering a new planning scheme amendment, ensuring broader views were sought, and improving communication with the community.

The ACC members now had a lot to do. Project management. Cost analysis. Financial modelling. Briefing lawyers and other advisers. Meeting and communicating with the council, the site vendors, the proposed developers and their architects, the Urban Land Corporation (ULC), Heritage Victoria, the National Trust, and officials from the Department of Infrastructure, the Ministry for the Arts and other official bodies.

They collated articles in the press, wrote letters to newspapers, rang talkback radio, took minutes, produced flyers and newsletters, lobbied politicians and attended meetings at Yarra Council and elsewhere. Chris O'Shaughnessy of estate agents Biggin & Scott supplied striking billboards that were put up, to great effect, along Johnston and Hoddle streets, on the bike path and in the front yards of businesses and private homes. Biggin & Scott also did the campaign's printing.

The ACC members researched government archives, ploughed through papers held by libraries and historical societies, and searched for evidence of the Indigenous heritage of the site. Such evidence would be invaluable when the campaign sought to communicate the convent's rich history and multifaceted value. It would also be crucial in planning future uses of the site.

The campaigners also sought evidence that in the mid-1970s Gough Whitlam and Dick Hamer, then respectively Australian prime minister and Victorian premier, had converted the convent site to Crown land, and that afterwards it had been changed back to private freehold status, perhaps recently by the ULC or perhaps at an earlier date, during the Dawkins-era university reforms of the 1980s. It was rumoured that Whitlam and Hamer, both of whom were from Kew, hadn't wanted the site to become factory land, like the Carlton & United Breweries site across the river. The ACC dispatched their researchers to scour library archives and the land titles office at Werribee. They searched for weeks but failed to find the original title or any other definitive evidence of the land's status.

Another thing the campaigners looked for, in collections such as those of the State Library, was evidence from other successful community activism. What might the ACC learn from prior campaigns? The search led to the striking discovery that nearly every other comparable effort had failed. Heritage campaigns hadn't halted the destruction of many of Melbourne's finest buildings. Community campaigns hadn't stopped public assets and public space from being privatised or turned over to closed development.

But the campaigners were able to learn a great deal from the failed campaigns, like the one to save Willsmere and the one to prevent the Formula 1 Grand Prix from being held at Albert Park. And they could learn from victories further afield in domains as diverse as Indigenous culture, community development and river health.

Using what they'd learned and what they hoped to achieve, the ACC wrote up the next generation of their proposal in the form of a 'vision document'. Lee produced a glossy version that described the solidifying option of an arts and cultural precinct at Abbotsford. The campaigners were exceptionally proud of their vision, now handsomely documented.

Lee's partner, Ming Tee, was a doctor, an audiologist, an air traffic controller and an amateur photographer. Lee produced a calendar that featured Ming's striking black-and-white photographs of the convent's features and vistas: Rosina, Sacred Heart, the kitchens, the cloister, the gallery, the view from the meadows and the Yarra.

Another highly effective document was a postcard that featured an exterior photo of the site taken from the riverside meadows, overprinted with a simple message: 'It would be a sin to ruin the Convent.' A new convent logo, with a cruciform 't' in 'convent', also made good use of the site's history.

Apart from being sources of pride for the ACC members, the vision document, calendar and postcard were surprisingly effective. They helped give the campaign more traction and visibility, and tended to turn up in unlikely and useful places. For example, after ACC members visited philanthropist Lady Marigold Southey, she displayed the 'sin' postcard prominently in her office, and one of the calendars was hung in the kitchen of the home of Premier Steve Bracks and his wife, Terry. The calendars had been on sale across Melbourne to raise funds for the campaign, and former Labor politician Barry Jones bought one at the Hill of Content bookshop on Bourke Street and drove straight to the Brackses' home in Williamstown, where he presented it as a gift. Jones and the Brackses were Labor Party friends; among other things, Terry had been Jones's electoral officer when Jones was a federal MP. On seeing the calendar, Terry's interest was piqued. She telephoned the ACC, a visit was arranged, and Kinross, Sally Romanes (a Melbourne-based lawyer who'd previously worked in a big law firm) and Lee took her on a two-hour rain-soaked tour of the site.

Once the ACC members had a profile in the media, they were trolled mercilessly on talkback radio, in newspaper letters pages, at council meetings and in the Victorian parliament. One councillor said they were 'just a bunch of basket weavers', and a state government minister dismissed them as 'chardonnay drinkers'. The members embraced these insults, adopting them as badges of honour. One time when Hilary Rankin called in live to ABC Radio's talkback presenter Jon Faine, she introduced herself by saying, 'Hi Jon, it's one of the basket weavers here.'

• • •

The St Heliers Working Party consisted of an independent chair, a Yarra councillor, two ACC representatives, two representatives from Australand and one from each of the Children's Farm, La Trobe University and the ULC. At its first meeting (on 23 March 1998) the working party decided to call for expressions of interest from parties with economically viable uses for a multipurpose site. It threw a wide net: possible uses for the site included hospitality, tourism, visual arts, performing arts, housing, education and 'therapeutic activities'.

The call for expressions of interest appeared in *The Age* in early April, and on 22 April, just two days before the EOI deadline, the ACC lodged its proposal for the conservation and restoration of the convent, and its use as a community arts and education precinct. The ACC was now deeply and directly implicated in a multimillion-dollar project. Potential tenants came forward, as did potential investors. Day by day, the stakes were rising and the campaign was becoming more sophisticated. The campaigners had the beginnings of a strong vision for the site, and had carefully assembled a skilled and agile group of people who knew how to think laterally and holistically. What else could they possibly need?

The answer was money. The ACC needed money.

In April 1998, an 'Abbotsford Convent Benefit Gig' at Collingwood Town Hall officially launched the ACC. More than 450 musicians, artists, volunteers, businesspeople and other supporters attended. The highlight of the night, which raised $3000 for the campaign, was a 'chook raffle' in which donated and discounted goods and services were haphazardly auctioned.

The next attempt to raise money had higher sights. In June 1998, using an adapted version of the vision document, the ACC applied for $10 million under the national Federation Fund Programme. Two politicians co-sponsored the application: the local federal ALP member and a Liberal senator whose office was in the City of Yarra. The ACC sent a copy of the submission to all state members of parliament, all federal MPs residing in Victoria, and all ministers whose portfolios related in any way to the alternative proposal. Despite these efforts, the application failed.

10
Flooded

THE ABBOTSFORD PENINSULA was prone to flooding—very severe flooding. In December 1856, the Yarra swept away much that had been built in nearby parts of early Melbourne:

> Rising fifty feet [15 metres] in two days, it swept in one tide over the south of the city to the sea, drowning many people and causing a quarter of a million pounds damage. It took entire houses to sea and wasted the farms of Collingwood and Kew. Even the shipping in the river had to wait till the level sank, the flood being so great that the course of the river could not be followed.

By 1863, memories of that flood had started to fade. The sisters bought Abbotsford House largely without fear of an imminent riparian disaster.

The grounds and paddocks of Abbotsford House were a key selling point in that purchase. In the convent's first year, the nuns and other women worked hard to establish a new garden on the site. 'Penny by penny', Mother Mary of St Joseph (Doyle) saved up £30 'in order that she might have the garden at Abbotsford laid out properly by an expert ... This was skilfully accomplished.'

In the new garden's terraces, the sisters carefully planted their plots. The results were soon evident: 'day by day the flowers opened out in soft and tender glory'. And then, in December 1863, the whole garden—all the terraces, all the plots—was washed away. Another great flood had devastated this part of Melbourne. Fearful about the nuns' safety, the people of the district 'gathered on the hills above, and kept watch and ward over the little community, ready at any moment to go to their assistance'.

The nuns rebuilt their garden, but just six years later the waters returned. In October 1869, *The Argus* reported that the low-lying lands around Abbotsford and the Johnston Street bridge had become submerged. At about 8 p.m. on Sunday 17 October, 'the water began to find its way into the dining room of Mr W. H. Smith, at the lower end of St Heliers Street … Following the course of the river down, the lower portions of the gardens of the Convent of the Good Shepherd are all under water, and a considerable amount of damage has been done.'

The *Mount Alexander Mail* provided a vivid chronicle of this 1869 flood:

> During the early forenoon of Saturday a moderate rainfall descended, but the middle portion of the day was dry. In the afternoon, however, the rain came down in torrents, and continued to do so throughout the night. About five o'clock on Sunday morning … the river was rising rapidly … From 5 o'clock until 7, and again from half-past 10 to half-past 1, the water is said to have risen more rapidly than it was ever known to do before, and by the hour last mentioned it had attained a height of five feet [1.5 metres] above its ordinary level. During the day it continued at about the same height, but about 7 p.m. it began to rise again, and overflowed the St Kilda road, a little beyond the south side of the Prince's Bridge … A large portion of the flats bordering the river was of course submerged, the water above the bridge, on the north bank, extending up to and inside the Suburban Railway embankment for a quarter of a mile [400 metres]. Up to midnight the water continued to rise but very slowly. [In Collingwood] considerable damage has been done … At Johnston Street bridge

> Mr Power's garden, and also the garden of the Convent of the Good Shepherd, at Abbotsford, have already suffered very much.

In 1878, flooding again caused considerable damage to the convent grounds. The *Wagga Wagga Advertiser* reported that the convent had 'again suffered considerably', and according to the *Weekly Times*:

> The appearance of the river at and around Studley Park on Sunday morning was very striking ... From Dight's Falls down to the Studley Park Bridge, and stretching beyond that to Richmond, the stream had nearly all the way trebled its width ... The river rose rapidly, and the current carried with it fallen logs, fencing, and every description of timber, which in its course submitted the supports of the bridges to a severe test. One of the wooden piles strengthening the support of a pillar of the Hawthorn Bridge was, in fact, broken in this way ... A two-storied brick house, situated about sixty yards [55 metres] from the river, at the bottom of St Heliers street, and occupied by Mr Moorfield, an engineer, was completely flooded out. The water approached the house in a marvellously short space of time ... and before all the furniture could be removed there was a depth of 6ft. [1.8 metres] on the ground floor. Mrs Moorfield and her children were at this time in the upper storey, unaware of their real danger, and when they descended they ran great risk of being drowned. A rope, however, secured to a portion of the fencing and the door of the house served to assist a man in rescuing them from their perilous position ... Further down the river, again, the damage done by the flood could be seen. About 100ft. [30 metres] of stone wall forming a portion of the western enclosure of the Abbotsford Convent was knocked down and completely carried away.

In July 1891, another 'Great Flood' damaged the convent grounds, destroying the orchard, much of the planted farmland and gardens, and fencing, hedges and paths. The cost of the damage was estimated to be over £500. According to *The Argus*, the rich topsoil was replaced with an unwelcome mixture of sand and rubbish. Overall, the grounds 'suffered to a very great extent':

> Situated in a sharp bend of the river, with the water coming well round on three sides of them, they were exposed to the full force of the flood and the water swept straight across the peninsula which is formed by the river, carrying all before it. The grounds, which have a river frontage of between 15 and 20 acres [6–8 hectares], had been planted with fruit trees, vegetables and cereal crops, and almost the whole of these have been destroyed. A plot of barley a few acres in extent, which was just ready for cutting, has been almost carried away, what remains of it being so completely flattened down and covered in sand as to be quite useless. Close down to the river there were two patches of Lucerne and oats, and of this not a vestige remains. In addition a large area was devoted to the purposes of a kitchen garden, which was well stocked with vegetables, and this also has been entirely spoiled. A portion of the ground had been set apart as a nursery for the propagation of seeds for transplanting, but this has fared no better than the rest … Almost the whole of the trees, consisting of fruit trees and ornamental ones, were razed to the ground, and many of them have been badly damaged and some ruined. The greater number have been replanted, but it is not likely that they will be of any use for the forthcoming season at least. Almost the whole of the fencing and hedges in the vicinity of the river have been either carried away or levelled to the ground, and the pretty belt of willow trees which skirted the bank of the river presents a very dilapidated aspect. The trees are almost entirely covered in debris.

Subsequent floods in 1901, 1911, 1916, 1923, 1934, 1935 and 1952 would again damage large areas of the convent gardens and grounds. In the 1923 flood, the 'turbulent, muddy Yarra' brought tree branches, fence pickets, sawn logs and other debris. When it reached the cliffs at Studley Park, it became 'a roaring, rushing torrent'. In another flood, the waters washed away the beloved rotunda and nearly reached the main buildings.

The 1934 flood devastated not only the orchard, the vegetable gardens, fences and outbuildings, but also the fountain that had graced the original gardens of Abbotsford House. Fortunately, the main convent buildings largely escaped the encroaching waters. After the 1935 floods, the sisters appealed for donations of vegetables to feed 'those whom the … institution shelters. Gifts and consignments of vegetables will be carried free if addressed [to] The Good Shepherd Convent, Abbotsford, Victoria Park railway station.'

11
The Great and the Good

THOUGH THE ABBOTSFORD Convent Coalition's application to the Federation Fund failed, the application process helped lift political awareness of the site and the campaign. It eventually led to further pledges of support from people in and near the state and federal governments.

The ACC members were always looking for new members who would happily donate time and ideas to the campaign. Very deliberately, they sought out people who could bring the precise skills the campaign needed as it progressed. And with equal focus, they sought out influential people who might help the campaigners' cause.

At 4 a.m. on the Saturday before Christmas 1998, Nigel Lewis was in Kew enjoying the tail end of a Christmas party, drinking red wine and eating a leftover cheese wheel and crumbled biscuits with Sally Romanes. The conversation turned to planning law, and particularly to the subject of urban encroachment and overshadowing along the Yarra.

Three days later, the Christmas hangovers had subsided and Lewis phoned Romanes. Another law firm had offered the ACC some pro bono input: would Romanes be willing to take a look at the firm and its offer? Romanes, Lewis and Jo Kinross went along to a meeting with the firm. The offer, on behalf of an unnamed party, was for a 'space for art within a private development' at Abbotsford. Kinross, Lewis and Romanes conveyed a clear reply: thanks, but no thanks. After this, Romanes was part of the campaign.

Accustomed to working in a rigid, pyramid-shaped hierarchy, Romanes found the ACC's structure refreshingly flat and flexible. The role of ACC convener rotated among the coalition members, and each meeting had a fluid agenda. She later described the campaign organisation as 'very organic, dynamic, with a democratic agenda on the whiteboard. A member would ask: "So what is today's agenda?"'

To the ACC, Romanes brought her expectations of how to run a large campaign for a large client, her methods of timetabling and Gantt charting, and an understanding of the size of the task now confronting the campaigners. At the next ACC meeting, she said they needed a business plan for their alternative proposal. Hilary McPhee agreed and said the ACC needed a 'name' to do the plan; otherwise, it would lack credibility in the planning process and when dealing with philanthropists and the government.

In the field of business cases and business plans, Price Waterhouse was a venerable and storied name. A former Price Waterhouse partner introduced the ACC to current partner Bill Russell, who headed the firm's property team. Romanes and Lewis went to meet him and his colleague Ray Harvey. Russell said he couldn't undertake the business plan himself as he'd previously advised the Urban Land Corporation in the process (around 1995, the ULC had considered a site-use proposal from Tony and Maureen Wheeler of Lonely Planet, and the ULC had asked Russell to comment on it), but he could mentor the campaign members and read drafts of their plans and submissions and other key documents.

Russell would turn out to be invaluable for the campaign, but in the meantime the issue of the business plan had to be solved in another way, by turning to another excellent name. David Cotterill of Sinclair Knight Merz (SKM) agreed to prepare it for a low bono fee.

Romanes also helped extend and mobilise the ACC's network of friends and supporters. Tony Lee did, too; he and others in the ACC were widely respected across Melbourne and maintained large networks. People who held the campaigners in high regard would be generous in their support.

From early in the campaign, the ACC had maintained a list of influential people who might help. It became known as 'The Great and the Good' and included such names as Dame Elisabeth Murdoch, Lady Marigold Southey, philanthropist Jeanne Pratt, celebrity restaurateur and food writer Stephanie Alexander, actor Sam Neill, the Wheelers, and *Vogue Australia* editor June McCallum. It also included politicians, bankers, academics and businesspeople.

Some of Pratt's Kew neighbours were on the list, as were artists and authors and former mayors, and the illustrious restaurateur Mietta O'Donnell. In the worlds of food and government and the arts, O'Donnell was well known and much loved. As an 'interested bystander', she helped bring others into the orbit of the campaign.

ALP luminary, author and former quiz-show champion Barry Jones was on the list. Several ACC members knew Jones, who in turn introduced them to Gough Whitlam. Jones introduced Romanes to Whitlam by saying: 'Sally has been working a lot on the convent', whereupon Whitlam kissed her hand.

Margot Foster saw the concrete value of the Great and the Good list: 'The list gave us access to expertise, and to star power.' It was regularly reviewed and updated, and every six months the ACC wrote to everyone on it. Among other things, that was a way to ensure the convent was a regular topic of conversation in homes and offices and at barbecues and dinner parties. The list became a roadmap: the basis for a series of organic visits with artists, philanthropists, politicians, community leaders and businesspeople, and a way to activate the nodal, flexible, fractal network that is called 'Melbourne'.

Dame Elisabeth Murdoch, the philanthropist and Murdoch matriarch, had supported the Royal Children's Hospital financially and served on committees there. Lewis knew the hospital's Dr John Colebatch, who knew Dame Elisabeth; and Lewis, Romanes and Colebatch went to see her at Cruden Farm on the Mornington Peninsula. They drove up to the house in Lewis's wife's Peugeot 306. Dame Elisabeth answered the door, noticed the Peugeot—she'd driven one herself for several years—and invited the visitors to enter. She put wood on the fire and Lewis set up the slide projector he'd brought. Dame Elisabeth watched the slideshow that described the convent precinct and buildings, and the idea of an arts and cultural precinct. Asking questions along the way—Lewis later described it as like being grilled by a QC—she was satisfied with the answers, and pledged a welcome $20,000 to pay for the SKM business plan.

A year later, a second meeting was organised. This time, Romanes and Lee made the trip to Cruden. The conversation got off to a good start (Dame Elisabeth referred to Lee as 'My dear young man'). Romanes had a connection to the Riverina—her family owned a sheep stud, 'Uardry', near Hay, and another large property, 'Yanga Station', near Balranald—and so did Dame Elisabeth. Her husband, for example, had invested in 1938 in the pastoral property 'Wantabadgery', near Wagga Wagga; and her son, Rupert, owned for a time the famous sheep property 'Wanganella', between Hay and Deniliquin. 'I love the Riverina,' Dame Elisabeth said. 'It feels as though you'll fall off the edge of the world.' Such shared connections helped build trust with her.

Another matter was even more important in trust-building. At this second meeting, Dame Elisabeth asked Romanes directly: 'Are you a professional fundraiser?'

'No.'

'What do you do?'

'I'm a lawyer.'

'And I'm an architect,' Lee said.

Satisfied with those answers, Dame Elisabeth addressed the matter at hand. 'I always think the early money is the most important,' she said. 'I can't be a magnificent donor, but I might be able to help a bit more. How about two hundred?'

Two hundred what? Romanes wondered silently.

Two hundred thousand dollars, it turned out.

Dame Elisabeth explained that much of her existing philanthropy was committed to recurring projects, but that she could help with projects she liked and that she thought would work.

Not long after this, another Murdoch family figure entered the picture. Roland Harvey, a children's book author, knew Lewis and Romanes. Together Lewis, Romanes and Lee went with Harvey to see Anne Kantor, daughter of Dame Elisabeth Murdoch and a sister of Rupert. It turned out that Romanes and Kantor already knew each other: as fellow members of a Feldenkrais class run by Mary Barlow, they'd met four or five years earlier while rolling around on the floor of Barlow's house. Through the Dara Foundation, Kantor made an initial contribution of $80,000 for the Abbotsford campaign.

Dame Elisabeth was certainly right about the importance of early money. Early support from people as credible as Dame Elisabeth and Kantor was vital to the campaign's prospects. The money was crucial, as was advice and other practical support from these leading philanthropists. From this point on, Dame Elisabeth was one of the most significant and enthusiastic supporters of the convent proposal. She made sure she was across every aspect and every stage of the campaign. A figure of enormous respect locally and internationally, she wasn't interested in being on the losing side of anything.

In a strategic masterstroke, the ACC enlisted Dame Elisabeth's help with inviting people to campaign events. On 20 June 1999, for example, an ACC benefactor event was held inside a barn at the Children's Farm and the invitations were sent out over Dame Elisabeth's signature. Billionaires Richard and Jeanne Pratt were among the Great and the Good supporters who attended, sitting down in the barn with the goats.

Lady Southey was another early supporter prepared to lend her name to the campaign. A prominent philanthropist and member of the Myer family, she would later be appointed as Victoria's lieutenant-governor. She was very taken with the convent gardens. On a tour some years later, she is said to have exclaimed, 'Get that ivy off those oak trees!'

The strong and visible connection with Dame Elisabeth lifted the standing of the convent campaign to a new level. It raised the stakes not just for the campaign but also for the developers and their supporters inside the government. Kantor's help would be just as important. Her financial contribution soon grew into a pledge of $2 million. Though initially this contribution wasn't publicised—the

ACC members were sworn to secrecy—they later sought and received Kantor's permission to tell the state government about this crucial endorsement of the alternative proposal.

Invaluable early pledges were also sought and received from other members of the Myer family and from others on the Great and the Good list. The fundraising showed how the campaigners' personal networks overlapped, and validated in spectacular fashion the benefits of a personal, tailored approach to seeking support. The campaigners used their vision document and other marketing materials as focal points for discussions with potential funders and supporters.

The most compelling drawcard was the convent itself. The site was fenced off and locked up, and as the contest to save it progressed, access became more and more difficult. Security guards patrolled the old grounds. For one open day, Australand logos were plastered on the facades of Rosina and other buildings, and there was a feeling that the developer had 'claimed' the site precipitously. But on the rare occasions when the campaigners were allowed to show people through the site, the impact was stunning and immediate, despite the guards and the logos.

'Whenever benefactors and politicians came to the convent, they got it right away,' Foster remembered. 'People always said the same thing: "It's like being in the country. All you can see is bushland." The precinct and the surrounding environment [were] everything.'

'The site spoke for itself,' said Sue Bannerman. 'It did the work of convincing people.'

Potential tenants made early commitments to the site and the ACC's proposal. What began as a trickle of prospective tenants became a river. The Steiner School, which had hosted the early ACC meetings in Nicholson Street, emerged as a potential anchor tenant in the future arts and education precinct.

Selected members of the Great and the Good list were asked if they would provide quotes for the campaign brochures. They replied with sincere and enormously useful words such as these.

> Dame Elisabeth Murdoch: 'This will be a wonderful place, unique to Melbourne and of lasting benefit to all Victorians.'

> Jeanne Pratt: 'Melbourne's cultural landscape will be enriched by this new arts and tourism complex. It complements and builds on the best of what Melbourne has to offer.'
>
> Janet McCalman, historian and author: 'The gains will be forever and they will be for all of us.'
>
> Lyn Williams, widow of painter Fred Williams: 'One of Fred's favourite sites was Yarra Bend where he painted the cityscape from Dights Falls. He particularly enjoyed the serenity of the old convent on the river bank, painting it several times.'

Lawyer, environmentalist and diplomat Simon Molesworth QC stated that the ACC project enjoyed the strong support of the National Trust. Hilary McPhee described the project as an opportunity that wouldn't come again, 'to save a great place and to bring together audiences, good food, training and young people'.

Committed participants who added their names to the brochures included the Australian Shiatsu College, Dance Compass, Handspan Theatre, the Handweavers and Spinners Guild, Kanga Manga Animation Studios, M3D Industrial Design Studio, the Melbourne School of Macrobiotics, Mietta's Queenscliff Hotel, REACH Adventure Tours, Roar Studios, Roland Harvey Studios, the Sophia Mundi Steiner School, St Martin's Youth Theatre, the Victorian Ceramic Group, Wild Moves Dance Company and radio 3MBS.

The brochures emphasised the community character of the proposal, but their authors were also careful to sprinkle commercial language throughout—words like 'synergies' and 'bankable'. The campaigners were keen, after all, to show that they weren't just 'chardonnay-drinking basket weavers'. The brochure contents were astute in other ways, too. One glossy ACC booklet featured a shirtless young man on a unicycle and, next to him, a stylish young woman with a whip. Above all, the impression from the materials was of credibility, resolve and unstoppable momentum. The ACC's Abbotsford solution was real, it was formidable, and it was locked in.

12
Life at the convent

THE CONVENT OF the Order of the Good Shepherd at Abbotsford was explicitly open to people of all religious denominations, and this was in keeping with the order's governing rule. In an 1864 pamphlet, the sisters announced that the Magdalen Asylum was 'open for the reception of females without distinction of country or creed, nor will it be sought to interfere with the religious principles of such as are not Catholics'. But the enterprise was fundamentally a Catholic one, and the nuns greeted with joy any conversions of non-Catholics into the embrace of the Roman church.

In early Melbourne the nuns confronted entrenched prejudices. Hostility to Catholics had deep roots. There were successful Catholics, to be sure, and prosperous Catholic communities, but Catholicism retained an association with poverty, and particularly Irish poverty. The order and the convent were important parts of a global enterprise, and this, too, caused suspicion among people who allied themselves with another global enterprise—the British Empire.

At the start of the twentieth century, Protestant activists published anti-Catholic missives that accused the Abbotsford Convent of 'sweating' its inmates and otherwise mistreating them. Some of the criticisms were well founded. Some sisters had racist and even eugenicist attitudes, and some were cruel and severe. The ethos at the convent was as much about custody as it was about support and rehabilitation. But many of the criticisms were fabricated, and many inmates experienced far better conditions at the convent than they could ever have had at home.

From the very beginning in Melbourne, the sisters wrestled with the question of how to make their convent viable. They took in sewing work: this would help them earn income and would give the penitents something practical to do besides working in the precarious, flood-prone garden. The nuns and their 'delicate fingers' became famous in Melbourne and further afield for their beautiful lace-making.

Money from sewing and lacework, however, wasn't going to be enough. The convent was growing rapidly. In its second year it admitted forty penitents (eight of these later left of their own accord, two were sent away for being 'incorrigible', and one died). A married couple joined the community as gardener and gatekeeper.

Most of the penitents were destitute and homeless. Once at the convent, they donned a specific uniform: a grey dress covered by a large apron. Many of them made 'an offering of their hair' as a sign of penance. Those unwilling to lose their locks tucked them under a white cap. As described by historian Catherine Kovesi,

> Most of the penitents wore a narrow dark blue ribbon on their chest with a medal of Mary attached to it. These were designated as 'aspirants', in other words, girls aspiring to behave in such a way as to merit being awarded the status of 'children' of Mary. Those attaining this level of behaviour were allowed to wear a broad, blue ribbon with the words 'Marie est ma Mère' embroidered onto it. Consecrated 'children' were differentiated still further by wearing a distinctive starched white bonnet … Penitent women were, as the nuns constantly emphasised, free both to enter and to leave. As the Abbotsford annalist described the situation: 'Some came and went several times. Some came so weak in mind and body they barely had time to make their peace with God before breathing their last. Some persevered for many years. Some joined the ranks of Consecrated Children.'

With energy and purpose, the sisters and their supporters raised funds for the convent. Sir John O'Shanassy and the Hon. Michael O'Grady lobbied the state government for a charitable grant of £200, to be directed to the Magdalen Asylum. Other eminent Melburnians organised a bazaar, which was held at St George's Hall on a grand scale and opened by Elizabeth Darling, wife of the governor of Victoria. Reports said that 'Madame Carandini sang the national anthem accompanied by a chorus of the Haymarket Company'. A 'resounding success', the bazaar raised £1400.

In 1864, to further support the financial needs of the community, the sisters decided to open a commercial laundry. In its first year the laundry raised the modest sum of £83/3/0. Soon, however, the service was indispensable to many Melbourne families and institutions. In 1865 it earned £330/10/7, and in 1866 £519/2/7. Melburnians would become accustomed to seeing the convent's laundry wagons and, later, delivery vans with 'Magdalen Asylum Laundry' in large letters on the side.

In the laundry the sisters worked alongside the Magdalens and other residents. The work was difficult and dangerous. Sister Mary of St Francis Regis (Flanigan) badly bruised her fingers in the steam mangle, and in May 1889 a laundry machine crushed the hand of Sister Mary of St Columba:

> she did not even scream as the machinery was loosened from her hand, walked back to the convent, as though nothing had happened, but fainted on arrival and subsequently had to have her hand amputated. Despite this, Sister 'bore her cross with admirable fortitude, offering her sufferings for the conversion of our loved Penitents to whom she is so devoted'.

Sometimes the sisters worked before the residents woke and after they went to bed. Speaking to Catherine Kovesi, Sister Helen Swiggs recalled that:

> we [the sisters] were working at midnight and I really thought [Sister] Vincent would die. Then we would be up at five, trying

> to get through the mountains of work, but we never got those mountains of work down—it was terrible.

Sister Felicitas Hanrahan told Sister Anne Dalton how the strictness of the rules, the injunction against talking about the past, the tough conditions of the laundry work and the values of the time could all come together in a terrible way for some of the women who sought shelter at the convent:

> Well, in hindsight now, I think I could have done a lot more had we known their circumstances. We didn't know one thing about them, which didn't make us as understanding as we could have been. I remember one day, a young girl was brought in—she would have been about fourteen or fifteen—and she was put at the mangle … Well, after a while she got tired or something, I suppose, and she went away and sat somewhere else … She was told to go straight back to the mangle. Now that child had been brought straight from having a miscarriage, and we didn't know … Well, you know, had you known … you'd have been more patient and more understanding … See, we were taught … that we were the nuns and we weren't allowed to even touch them. That made you sort of distant.

Melbourne at this time was filling up with abandoned and destitute children. In 1864, the parliament passed the Neglected and Criminal Children's Act, which allowed for the establishment of government and voluntary 'industrial schools' and 'reformatories'. (Industrial schools provided trade training to 'neglected' children, while reformatories were for 'criminal' children. These two categories were frequently blurred.) When children were found 'begging in the streets, in the company of criminals or in brothels or … without a home or income', the police could bring them before the courts and have them committed to an industrial or reformatory school. Parents could likewise ask for 'uncontrollable' children to be committed to an industrial school. Many poor families took up this opportunity.

Bishop Goold saw an opportunity for Abbotsford to host a reformatory for young women prisoners and an industrial school for destitute children. The Government Reformatory for Criminal Girls, Abbotsford, opened in October 1864. Children at the Reformatory School served sentences of one to five years, but stayed on until they could be placed 'with respectable families'. By the end of the first year, six girls had been admitted. The Industrial School was for children who'd been deserted or were otherwise not under the control of their parents, and were 'in danger of becoming wicked'. Though not convicted of any crimes, the Industrial School children were referred to as 'inmates' and their presence at Abbotsford as 'imprisonment'.

For the wards and inmates of the Convent of the Sisters of the Good Shepherd, daily life 'behind the wall' was all about hard work, holy observance, segregation, rigid rules and a rigid routine. It was a life lived largely apart and in secret, punctuated by special occasions such as bazaars and visits by the archbishop. Great efforts were made to occupy the minds and bodies of the reformatory and industrial school inmates, who, like the penitents, weren't permitted to speak of their former life or discuss their past misdeeds. Intimate friendships, too, were forbidden.

In 1869, Melbourne's *Argus* published the timetable of some of the younger inmates of the Good Shepherd institution:

6 to 6.30: Rise, dress and make beds.
6.30 to 6.45: Morning prayer.
6.45 to 7.15: Breakfast.
7.15 to 8: Mass.
8 to 8.30: Talking whilst doing work.
8.30 to 9: Silence, work continued.
9 to 10: Reading.
10 to 10.30: Monday and Thursday, grammar and geography; Tuesday, Wednesday, and Friday, dictation.
10.30 to 11: Writing.
11 to 11.30: Arithmetic.
11.30 to 12: Sing canticle, sewing.

12 to 12.30: Dinner.
12.30 to 1.30: Recreation.
1.30 to 2: Singing canticle, silence, sewing, &c.
2 to 2.30: Lecture.
2.30 to 3: Study.
3 to 3.30: Sewing and other work.
3.30 to 4: Talking whilst doing work.
4 to 4.30: Religious instruction, catechism.
4.30 to 5.45: Household work, &c.
5.45 to 6: Recite the Rosary.
6 to 6.30: Supper.
6.30 to 8: Recreation.
8: Night prayers, and retire in silence to bed.

On Sunday evenings, the sisters and their wards formed religious processions that wended their way through the grounds, singing hymns and carrying banners.

The 'industrial children' were kept apart from the reformatory children except in the schoolroom, and even there they were segregated 'in different parts of the classroom'. Claud Farie was the government-appointed inspector of reformatories. In an 1867 report, he wrote that the reformatory and industrial children were 'kept in separate dormitories at night, one large ward being set apart for each school, and one of the Sisterhood sleeps in a room adjoining each of the wards, with a window between for inspection, so that the children may be said to be under supervision by night as well as by day'.

Separation was maintained even in church. As *The Advocate* reported in 1871, 'The eastern transept … is intended for the penitents on the ground-floor, while the gallery overhead will be for the children of the Industrial Schools.' There were other degrees of separation as well. Children sent to the Industrial School by their parents or guardians occupied a section known as the Preservation Class. The 'preservates' were parentless and neglected girls who had been placed in the care of the sisters by parents or relatives, or by conscientious members of the public. Several were the daughters of women in the penitents' class.

Abbotsford House, c. 1860
(Collingwood Local History Photograph Collection)

The Magdalen Asylum from Studley Park Hill, 1869
(State Library Victoria)

THE GOOD SHEP

Abbotsfor

Top: The Convent of the Good Shepherd, Abbotsford, c. 1910
(State Library Victoria)
Above: The church erected in memory of Mother Mary of St Joseph (Doyle), 1889. Part of the original 'Abbotsford House' is visible on the left.
(Good Shepherd Archives)
Left: Magdalen Asylum, Abbotsford, c. 1880
(Good Shepherd Archives)

Convent of the Good Shepherd, 1902
(Good Shepherd Archives)

Portrait of Mother Mary of St Euphrasia Pelletier, c. 1825
(Good Shepherd Archives)

Bridget Doyle, aged about 22, shortly before joining the Sisters of the Good Shepherd in 1858
(Good Shepherd Archives)

Pupils at St Euphrasia's Day School, 1915
(Good Shepherd Archives)

Residents of the Magdalen Asylum in their courtyard
(Good Shepherd Archives)

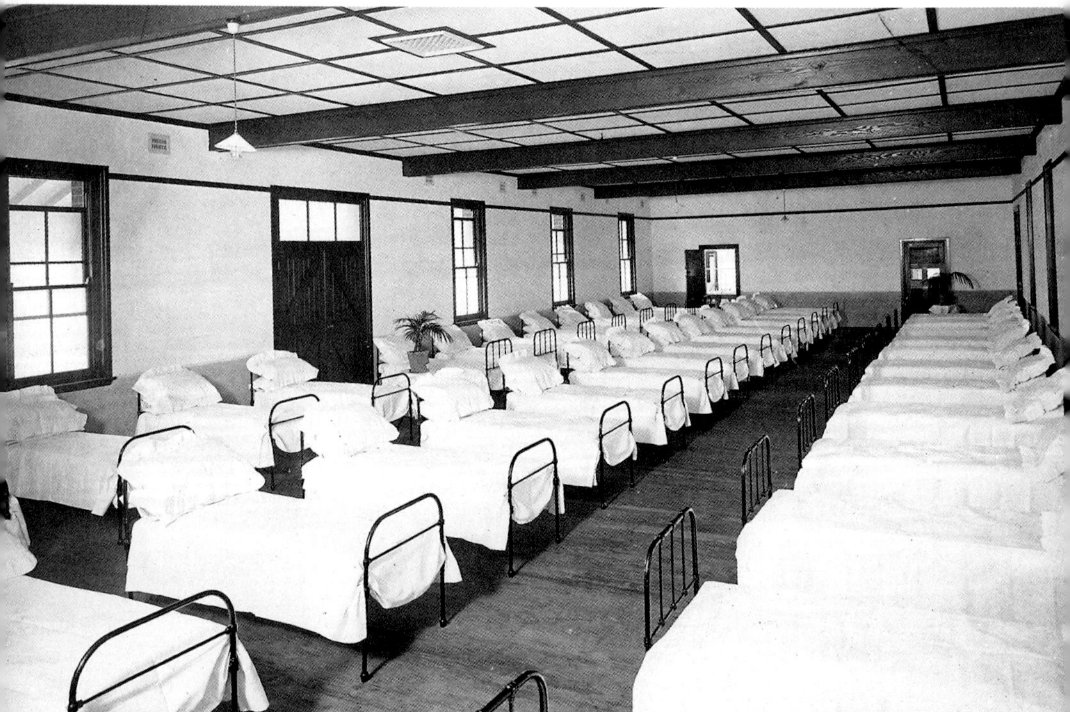

Dormitory in Sacred Heart (the Magdalen Asylum)
(Good Shepherd Archives)

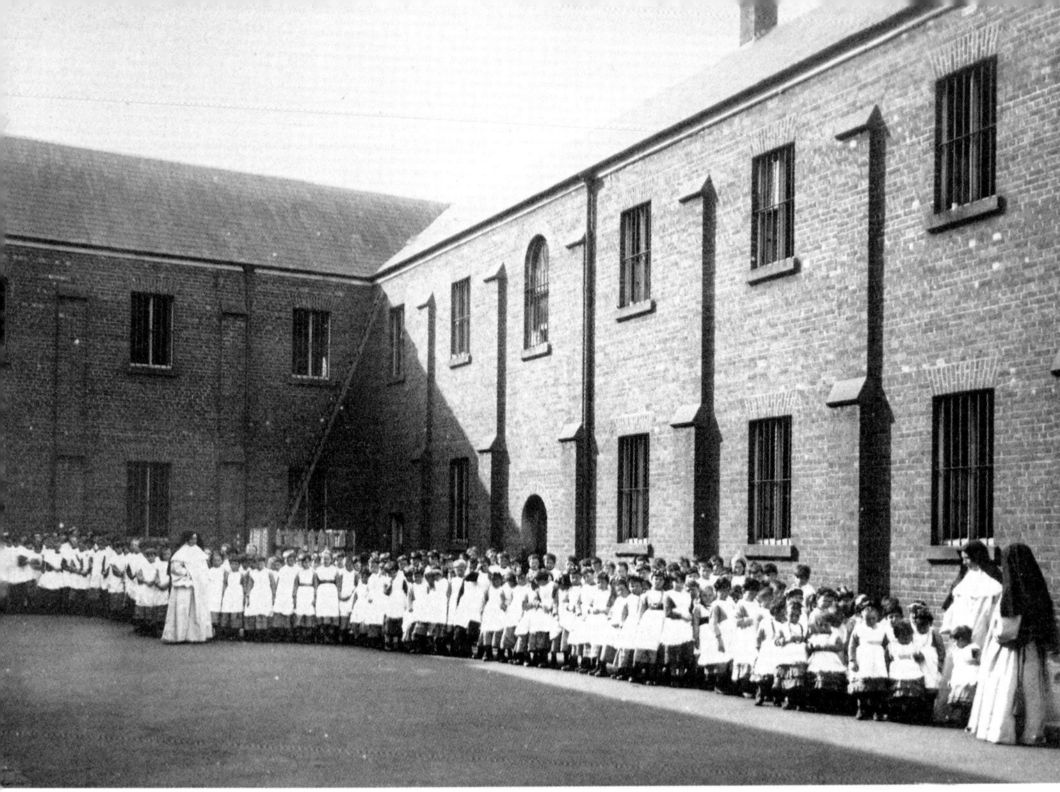

Pupils of St Joseph's Industrial School, 1889
(Good Shepherd Archives)

Typing class at Our Lady of Lourdes Commercial School
(Good Shepherd Archives)

The Convent's old ironing room, under the direction of Sister Mary of St Therese (Sullivan)
(Good Shepherd Archives)

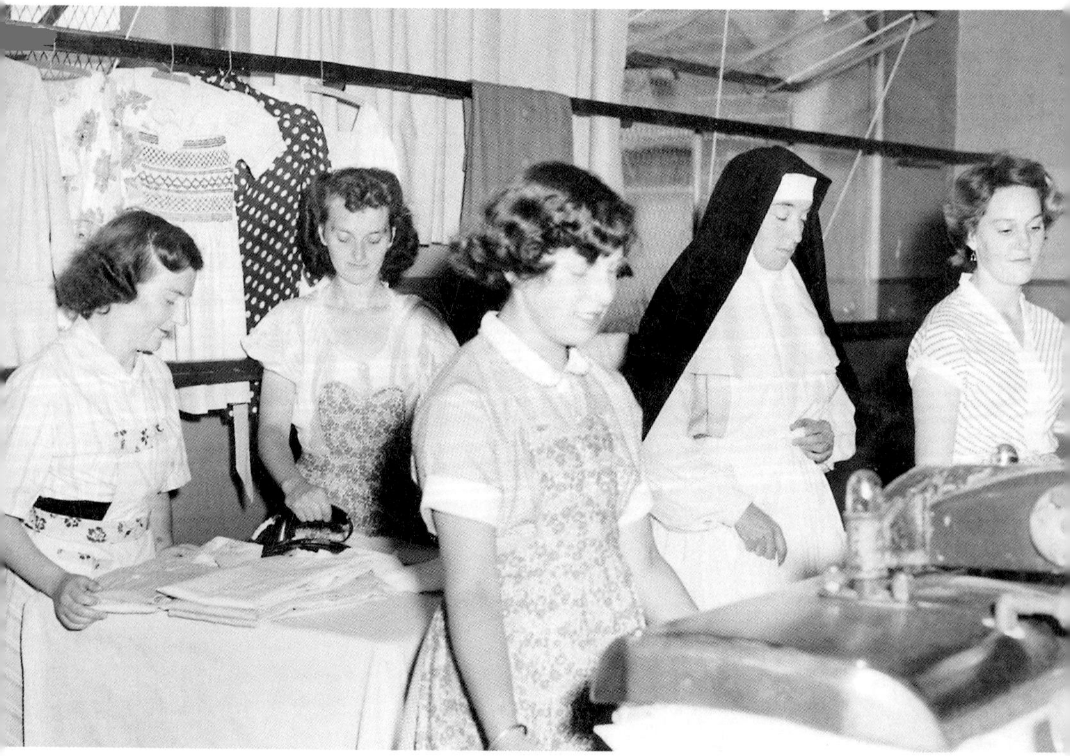

The Convent's new ironing room, under the direction of Sister Mary of St Aloysius (Crawford)
(Good Shepherd Archives)

The sisters managed the industrial and reformatory girls according to a detailed set of rules. Devised in Angers, written in French and applied in Melbourne, the rules deliberately connected Abbotsford to a longstanding tradition. Mary Euphrasia emphasised loyalty, continuity and adherence to the order's rules: 'When, my dear daughters, you go by Holy Obedience to another foundation, never fail to take the Mother House as your model, and not any other house even if, to you, it seems perfect.'

In 1870, the sisters' industrial and reformatory schools received special support under an act of parliament: £13 a year for supporting 'each female criminal or neglected girl committed to the institution by the courts of justice'. *The Advocate* reported that the sisters were performing an important public service: 'The industry and the resources of the Nuns, and the generosity of the public, apart from the Parliament, are taxed to support these children, who, if they were in Government schools of Sunbury, Prince's Bridge, &c., would cost the State double the amount given to the Nuns.'

The convent was subject to an official inspection regime that reported to parliament. The report of 1872 on 'Industrial and Reformatory Schools' commended 'the mode and merits' of the convent for the industrial and reformatory discipline of the female children in its care. Happily for the state, this high standard was achieved at a comparatively low cost:

> In the Government establishments the gross cost per head for maintenance in the Industrial and Reformatory Schools appears to be: Melbourne £25/2, The Nelson £21/8/4 … In Abbotsford, under the Sisters of the Good Shepherd, £12 13s 9¾d.
>
> This disparity in the allowance for the maintenance, the clothing, the education, and other requisites shows convincingly that Catholic charity is burdened enormously, and that if the State funds for carrying out the Neglected and Criminal Children's Act were fairly meted out, the Nuns at Abbotsford should be paid at the rate of twenty-one pounds sterling at least a head for the children so well and faithfully tended by them.

> In the suggestions for the reform of our reformatory institutions one would expect to find a remedy for the Nuns of the Good Shepherd, who, out of their straitened resources, are obliged to find and expend over a thousand pounds annually to maintain the children committed by the State to their benign custody … It is not alone this oppressive annual burden that is imposed upon the Nuns, for they are also obliged to incur increasing expenditure out of their own ways and means for providing houses, schoolrooms, playgrounds, and other buildings and places necessary for their good and effective work.

In 1891, when the commissioners of the Charities Commission visited the Magdalen Asylum, they were struck by 'how much can be done by women under the supervision of their own sex. The boiler-house gave a practical exemplification of this fact. The engine was found to be entirely looked after by women, who light the fires, clean the machinery and do all other necessary work without men's assistance.'

The applause, though, wasn't universal. In 1885, Mary Ann Stafford, a fifteen-year-old inmate of the convent, died from typhoid fever in the Melbourne Hospital. The girl's mother, a resident of Church Street off Little Lon, alleged that the sisters had mistreated her 'quiet, inoffensive' daughter. Police inquiries followed.

Mary Ann had been at the convent for a month prior to her death. According to her mother, 'She was then in excellent bodily health, had never had a fit, and had not any mark of violence about her.' Then the convent wrote to advise her that Mary Ann was ill, and she rushed to her daughter's side:

> Upon reaching the convent, the mother 'found the girl lying in a filthy state in bed, unable to speak. Both her eyes were very black, there was another mark of violence on her nose, and a further examination disclosed another severe bruise on one of her groins; in fact, to use the mother's words, "she was black and blue"'.

Once at Church Street, Mary Ann 'recovered somewhat, and told her mother that she had been beaten by a nun, and then by two young women, and put into a bath, and then into the bed, where she was found by her mother as described'. After being seen by a doctor, she was taken to the hospital where she died. A post-mortem examination determined that the immediate cause of death was typhoid fever and inflammation of the girl's lungs. At a subsequent coronial inquest, a jury cleared the sisters, finding 'there was nothing to show that the deceased was ill-treated at the convent'. But this sad episode weighed heavily on the convent and its reputation—and further distress would follow.

In 1903, Reverend John Hosking, secretary of the Protestant Union of Collingwood, wrote to advise the Collingwood Council that the union had passed unanimously a resolution:

> That the union respectfully ascertain from the Collingwood City Council a reason as to why the Roman Catholic laundry, convent and landed property at Abbotsford are exempt from municipal and water rates, as such a great concession to any industrial and religious body is an injustice to the ratepayers of Collingwood; also, that as there are nearly 100 hands employed in the laundry aforementioned, the council be asked for information as to why that institution (viz., the laundry) is exempt from the Factories Act, especially as little or no wages are paid there for the work done, and a great many excellent workpeople, females especially, are debarred from procuring the means of an honest livelihood.

Later that year, at an event in Footscray, Reverend Hosking continued the campaign against the Magdalen Laundry:

> He stated that that institution used millions of gallons of water, and never paid a penny in rates for it … The Magdalen Laundry had the contract for the Melbourne Hospital washing at 1/6 per dozen. The manager of a laundry told him that a firm in Melbourne paying the minimum wage could not do the work for less than 3/ per dozen.
>
> Was it right that the Magdalen Laundry should be allowed to carry on business without paying rates and without being made

to conform to the Factories Act? The Government gave £1000 every year to the Magdalen Asylum. In addition to there being a laundry there was a boot factory, also 30 cows and several horses. One could look over the hill near the institution and see women driving drays and carting soil from one part to the other. That kind of thing should not be tolerated in a Protestant country. It was very repugnant in the Protestant mind to see women subjected to such work as driving those carts. There were over 300 employed at the laundry. These women did not get wages, but when they left they received £1 and a few articles of clothing, and they were asked to stay a few weeks longer as a thanksgiving offering. (Laughter.) The place occupied sixty acres [actually 20 acres, or 16.2 hectares] on land in the municipality of Collingwood, and was exempted from rates. If he were a ratepayer in Collingwood he would make a jolly row. (Laughter.) He was tempted to buy an allotment, even if it was only about 2 feet. (Laughter.) As a ratepayer he would then ask the Council why it exempted sixty acres from rates. He once asked the Collingwood Council that question as secretary of the Protestant Union, but the communication was received with contempt. There were Roman Catholic detectives who got hold of any tipsy women they saw and ran them into these places, and got them to work in the laundry. That was how these institutions were replenished.

Some of these women broke their hearts staying in there and some their heads, for the van from the Kew Asylum was a frequent visitor to the place. He would like to get a return showing the number of patients in the Kew Asylum who came from the Abbotsford institution. It would be an eyeopener. It was a very strange thing that Labor members, who were very strong on the Factories Act, kept quiet on this convent business. He was pleased to see that there was one brave man, Mr Alex Ramsay, MLA, who was prepared to take this matter up. But Mr Ramsay got very little support from other members of the State Parliament, and practically stood alone in this matter. When the matter of the Magdalen Laundry was mentioned, sometimes one was told that

> the Salvation Army people were also exempt from the Factories Act. He had found that the Salvation Army printing establishment was under the Factories Act. Besides taking in women and putting them to laundry work, the Roman Catholic institution also received children into the orphanage and taught them to work.

Via the sympathetic *Advocate*, the sisters made their defence against this outbreak of sectarian hostility. Asked by the newspaper about competition with other laundries, the Reverend Mother replied:

> Competition was unknown in Melbourne in the laundry trade until 1891; yet the Magdalen Asylum had been doing the work of the city, large hotels, leading private families, etc, etc, since 1863. After the 'boom' period, followed the great depression, and consequently, numbers turned to laundry work. A large steam laundry was built at Yarraville. The proprietors ... imported machinery of the newest style from America ... They lowered the prices to such an extent that though several took up the industry all failed. Another business firm in Melbourne, having machinery for its trade, thought it could do laundry work without further cost. Prices were lowered to 4d a dozen, and contracts taken for 25 per month that we had at 75 and 80 per month. A couple of years ago the cry against the Magdalen Asylum was raised, and the use of free water criticised. The papers went so far, and the correspondence at the Board of Works against the asylum was so great, that a deputation of impartial representatives visited the convent to make enquiries. Letters from customers were shown to them. One was from a hospital for which we did the washing at 1s per dozen. The largest laundry in Melbourne offered to do it for 6d a dozen, and so got it. The institution was publicly blamed, while other laundries were able to do as they pleased.

The Reverend Mother emphasised the social purpose and value of the laundry, as was demonstrated especially during the 1890s depression, and its minimal impact on the commercial industry:

> We never interfere with the public trade. We do not compete, as the inmates are not equal to it. We try to secure, in an honourable way, work to help to support the inmates, and to teach them to earn a living for themselves when they leave the institution, either in public laundries or in private families.

When the specific question was put to her—was the convent 'sweating' its inmates?—the Rev. Mother Provincial replied:

> By no means. We know that report has gone abroad through inmates who go from one institution to another, and spend a time in gaol. They do not believe in doing any work, and foolishly raised some complaint, either of food, work, or unkindness, to justify their action in going away. As a rule, such women never do a day's work; but, in or out of a home, they create sympathy for themselves where they can get a hearing. Generally speaking, the young girls and women who come to Abbotsford are genuine in their intention of doing better, and, when they find, after one, two or three failures that they cannot get on, they prefer to end their days in the institution rather than be a burden on public charity. Such a class love work and take great interest in it.

Why shouldn't the laundry fall under the Factories Act?

> Because the inmates are not able to compete. Owing to weak and broken down constitutions, unsteady dispositions, and the fact of coming here to be reclaimed, it would be degrading on them if they were subject to inspection. The institutions would no longer be a refuge, and many timid and gentle persons would never have the courage to come as they now do.

Did the convent laundry have fifty carts? No, only twelve, across three institutions. Did a boot factory operate at the convent?

> It is a well-known fact that we make house shoes for inmates and repair some of the boots and shoes. Many of the inmates are not

> equal to laundry work, and we find any employment possible to keep them occupied. We, however, … buy a very large number for general use. For the sake of economy we do all we can to save expense. The Sisters do all the supervision, but we have to employ workmen, and we pay fifteen such, between laundry, carpentering and gardening, besides the amount spent on tradesmen, repairs, etc.

Were other works of charity carried out at the convent?

> Yes. We have a primary school, with an average attendance of 270 on the roll. They pay very little and over 100 pay nothing at all. We understand those girls would cost for teaching £4 per head. Then we have to keep, feed, clothe and educate 241 preservatives, including orphans, neglected and imbecile children … Much of these should be on the State—as acknowledged by the late Inspector of Charities, and by all Parliamentary and other visitors—if we did not give them our time and our labour to keep them, as well as to give them a good education. When over school age they are trained to household duties, and prepared for service. We have no difficulty in finding homes, and our wards are to be found in all the States doing and earning well.

Did the sisters have any objection to a visit by an external inspector?

> Not the least objection. It is well known that the institution is open to inspection and the Sisters are only too glad to receive advice and assistance in the way of improvement, and for the additional comfort of the inmates.

The sectarian gibes continued, nourished by convent scandals interstate and abroad. A Melbourne lecture by the Reverend Canon Berry on 'Reformation Heroes' turned to the question of convent industries and 'their exemption from factories regulations':

> Canon Berry at the outset referred to certain statements made by Archbishop Carr, as reported in 'The Age' of Monday. He, this

> speaker, had not, he said, made a 'dead set' upon the Abbotsford Convent, but merely made an urgent suggestion that its industrial department should be brought under inspection and regulations like other factories. That was only a reasonable thing. The facts which he used in support of his contention were brought from 'distant countries', namely France and England, for the reason that the Abbotsford Convent belonged to the same order as those which had been the chief offenders in France and England against common humanity, and would, therefore, presumably be worked up on the same methods and on the same system. If only for the mere vindication of its own character the Abbotsford Convent ought to invite and welcome regular inspection. But the facts were drawn, not only from England and France, but also from New South Wales. The sworn testimony of an ex-inmate of the convent industrial school in Manly showed that the same kind of abuses which in France had so shocked the world had begun to show themselves in Australia. He had in his remarks only advocated for Australia what Sir Godfrey Lushington, late Under Secretary of the Home Office, had advocated for England, as was shown in an article by him which appeared in the 'National Review' for last month.

In 1905, five Protestant women took it upon themselves to visit the convent unannounced. Sydney's Protestant newspaper *The Watchman* reported the inspection in granular, fascinating and triumphant detail (see pages 153–8). Though infused with awkward misunderstandings and sneering arrogance, the account of the visit provided a priceless document of life in the convent at the start of the twentieth century. It describes the convent's security arrangements and religious imagery, along with the 'handsome' rugs and fittings, the demeanour and clothing of students, the sleeping arrangements, convent baking (the biscuits and cakes 'looked nice'), the laundry and other manual activities ('young girls wheeling barrows').

More obviously overt sectarian attacks followed. *The Watchman* published a statement allegedly made by an escaped inmate:

I, Ella Laughton, was born at Penhurst, September 2nd, 1875, and will be twenty years of age next September. My father was killed in the July flood, and my mother died about two years ago in the Melbourne Hospital. I have no relations, only my grandmother's sister. I have been to service, but this distant relation, as I call her, asked me about ten months ago to go for a tram ride, and, getting out of the Abbotsford tram, escorted me into the convent without knowing it was a convent, until I was told so. I was then asked by the nuns what I could do, so told them I had always been at service. I was then asked if I would stop there for two or three months, as it would do me good to be there, so I agreed. When the three months lapsed I asked permission to go out, and was refused, and told it would do me good to be there, and I received this same answer every time I asked to go out. I did no wrong in there, and did no wrong before I was taken in the convent, so determined to escape when I got the chance. I told the nuns that I would try and escape, and did so on Sunday morning, June 4th. 1905. I thought I would go towards Richmond, and try and find this distant relation, but failed. While in the convent I was informed by a young girl that mentioned she stayed with an old lady in Otter street, Collingwood, and had a daughter named Lizzie. I asked where this street was, as I thought they may allow me to do my hair, and give me an old hat to wear, as I had none on my head. I found this street, and, on making inquiries, I related my story of escape to a young girl, she informed her mother, and this person received me in her home, and, having been attended to by her, I was kindly asked to remain, which I did. I have been asked by this lady to remain in her home as one of her daughters, and to be called as such, or to remain until I got right situation. I consented to stay with this lady, and feel comfortable and happy.

I was working in the convent for nearly nine months in the ironing room. I am a Protestant and was obliged to go to mass, also to catechism, and also to witness all in their religious service. They wanted me to go to the confessional box, and tried very hard to get me to go, but they did not succeed. Many Protestant girls try and

> escape. Three or four escaped the same week as I did. One girl in particular, from Kensington, has been in there four or five years, against her will, and would do anything to get away, and made a number of attempts to escape. There are some girls who are there for life, and they are kept constantly on the watch to prevent any getting away, or attempting to escape.

The Watchman advised that the young woman was now being well cared for by a member of one of the staunchly Protestant Orange ladies lodges. 'This good sister took her in and gave her a home for as long as the girl liked, and also secured employment for her. The dress she escaped in, and the little white cap, and all the clothing worn at the convent are numbered. These will be kept as a memento of her nine months' incarceration.'

The Advocate countered with a decidedly different version of Laughton's story. Far from being an orphan duped into entering the convent, Ella was a former inmate of Melbourne Gaol who, upon her release from prison, asked to be taken in by the nuns at the Abbotsford Convent, agreeing to stay for twelve months to learn laundry work. She subsequently ran away. Her statement was witnessed by 'T.A.R.—, J.P., who so modestly refrained from disclosing his identity in this unsavoury case'. *The Advocate* exposed the justice of the peace as 'T. A. Rogers, the accredited representative of the "Watchman" in Melbourne, and whose name is so frequently mentioned in the paper in connection with several Orange functions'.

In August 1906, Reverend George Tregear of the Collingwood Methodist Mission addressed an Orange gathering at the Collingwood Town Hall. He painted a terrible picture of the enterprise whose leaders owed 'primary loyalty to the Pope'. Tregear's lurid criticisms drew a direct response in the form of a letter to the editor of *The Age*:

> Sir, I respectfully beg to inform you that I was an inmate of that grand institution, namely, the Abbotsford Convent, for a period of ten years, and most certainly the Rev. Mr Tregear has been, I am sure, misinformed. I never saw during the ten years I was there,

the inmates so sparingly fed as Mr Tregear states. They have to work hard, but they (the inmates) are undoubtedly well clothed and fed, and have good beds to sleep on; in fact, I was so surprised by the Godlike manner these poor souls (the inmates) were guided to the right path that I, who came from a Scotch Presbyterian family, became, I am happy to say, a Roman Catholic from pure conviction, without once being asked to do so. I have known the nuns of Abbotsford for a period of 28 years, and I have known cases upon cases who came to the convent for assistance, and I have never known anyone, irrespective of creed or colour, who ever went away without being liberally assisted. Having been so long associated with these holy women, I feel so grieved that I could not refrain from writing to you, Sir.

Yours, etc., (Mrs) Isabella Jessop. Stafford-street, 22nd January.

Further evidence was provided by a 'surprise visit' made by the official inspector of charities, Francis Short, who was in turn instructed by Thomas Bent, the premier of Victoria, to inquire into the charges made by Tregear. At the end of January 1907, Bent released Short's report. At the time of the inspection, Abbotsford had 360 inmates and a financial deficit of £1,507 'on account of building'. The report concluded that 'The cost per bed during last year was £21/17, which is low. The institution is managed economically.' As to the 'special charges' made against the convent, the inspector verbally informed the premier that there were no grounds for them.

The premier later took exception to the statement that he had sent the inspector to pay a 'surprise visit' to the convent, as he 'did not do that sort of thing'. He asserted, 'It is a fact, however, that, like all that officer's visits, it was unexpected, and there are the best of reasons why the visits of such an officer should not be specially prepared for by the institutions he is to visit.'

According to *The Advocate*, Tregear now changed tack:

Speaking at the Collingwood Mission meeting on Sunday, the Orange ranter said that he had written to the Certificated

> Enginedrivers' Association, asking if it was right that a woman should work at driving an engine, and the reply he received stated: 'We are aware of the conditions obtaining at the Abbotsford Convent, and decline to lend ourselves to any party intent on stirring up sectarian strife in our midst.'

In light of his repeated attacks on the Abbotsford Convent and other Catholic institutions, and especially his repeated fabrication of 'rescue' stories, Melbourne police described Tregear as 'a fanatical crank'.

But criticisms of convent industries and the treatment of inmates would continue into subsequent decades. For example, newspaper articles in 1918 accused the Good Shepherd of overworking their wards, monopolising Melbourne's laundry trade, and undercutting prices while simultaneously reaping huge profits. At a 1922 ceremony to bless and open St Anthony's Home for Destitute Children at Kew, Archbishop Dr Daniel Mannix specifically addressed some of the criticisms levelled at the convent:

> Dr Mannix said that women and girls housed there were put to useful work in the laundry. He denied Sunday work took place at the convent, and said the laundry at Abbotsford was open to regular Government inspection. Reasonable people should be satisfied when the Government officers were. So far from a huge profit being made out of the industry at Abbotsford, he knew that the institution had a deficit of several thousand pounds. The convent laundry adhered to schedule rates, and did not undercut in prices, and because it did not it had lost many orders.

As late as 1952, there was criticism that girls of working age laboured in the laundry for no wages and 'alongside mental derelicts'. But the Melbourne *Herald* published a defence of the convent, its sister institutions and their work:

> The explanation in each instance was that the girls' work could not always be relied upon and that the institution could not afford to pay wages, as it was feeding and clothing them …

I found the physical condition of inmates good. They were well fed, medical attention was regular, and many places have their own dentist's chair.

There are varying standards of amenities—depending largely on how many voluntary organisations help a particular home.

Educational facilities for children up to 14 mostly are good. Many religious institutions staff their own schools ... At the Convent of the Good Shepherd, Abbotsford, girls are taught music, typing, sewing, cookery, mothercraft, ballet and dramatics. Those with talent are encouraged to go on to secondary education.

13
The legacy

IN MARCH 1998, Australand put its original plans for the redevelopment on ice. In their place, the developer chose six firms of architects to participate in a design competition. Then, in June, it held an open day at the convent to reveal the plans of the three shortlisted firms.

There was a fourth vision on show at the open day: the vision of the Abbotsford Convent Coalition, presented as a series of foam-core display boards showing aspects of the ACC's arts and cultural vision. ACC members were on hand to explain the proposal's philosophy and features. This all took place inside the old Linen Room in one of the convent buildings. Outside the convent boundary, near the main entrance on St Heliers Street, the coalition set up an information table to reach more people. Many joined the ACC then and there and offered their help. Membership rose to the extraordinary figure of 400.

The location of the ACC table at the open day was the subject of some controversy, and the target of some skulduggery. Putting the table at the main entrance would have made sense if that was going to be the only gate open on the day. But as Charlotte Allen later recalled, 'after a few hours we were told that Australand had opened the Clarke Street gate [around the corner] and also the one between the chapel and the main gate, meaning lots of people were missing our table!'

Crucially, people at the open day noticed that the ACC proposal involved hardly any changes to the convent's built spaces and grounds. Each building told a story, and with the ACC option those stories would be protected. The Australand options, in stark contrast, would in-fill floors, break the tall windows and destroy the integrity of the buildings. The bakery, the laundries, the light wells, the timber trusses: people saw that these would go. Above all, the wonder of the site would be lost.

The open day was a turning point in the campaign. Allowing the campaigners to exhibit their alternative proposal was a tactical error on the part of the redevelopment proponents, giving the ACC crucial airtime and their proposal greater status. The alternative vision was on at least the same level as the three shortlisted 'mainstream' options. People rushed to get behind the ACC option.

'Whenever the ACC spoke of the plans,' Sue Bannerman said, 'the people listening lit up.' The campaign members were ecstatic.

In other ways, too, the open day was crucially important. Of the hundreds of people who visited the site that day, many arrived early and were holding photos of themselves as girls and young women. They were former convent residents returning for the first time, equipped with photographic means to connect themselves to the site and to other former residents.

The event opened the way for hundreds of poignant moments. The visitors were allowed to enter spaces that had been strictly out of bounds during the highly regulated and tightly segregated convent era. Now, former inmates could explore areas that had once been accessible only to the sisters or the archbishop. One remembered her girlhood at the convent. She used to have to bring tea to Archbishop Mannix, and was terrified each time, and she wasn't allowed to touch the banisters because they had to be kept spotlessly clean.

The former residents could explore the previously sequestered belltower and balconies, and the exquisite secret chapel in Sacred Heart. They could stride up the grand staircases and run their hands along those formerly untouchable banisters. And the most striking thing of all: they could meet.

Two former residents at the open day had seen each other decades before, sitting in opposite sections of the Church of the Immaculate Conception. During the church services they'd sometimes made eye contact, but they'd never actually met. Now, at the open day, they were finally able to speak to each other and share their stories and their understanding of life behind the wall.

Some of the former Abbotsford residents had happy memories of the place; others' memories were sad or bitter. As the former nuns, novices, penitents, inmates, students and orphans shared stories during the open day, more than one wall came down. The ACC members for their part discovered further layers of the convent's history, and began to understand the scale of the legacy and the responsibility that a future steward of the convent would bear.

• • •

At the open day and subsequent public events—including a meeting on a freezing-cold night at the old Collingwood Town Hall—there was strong backing for the ACC proposal and strong opposition to the Australand option. This balance of views would continue into the next stage of the planning process.

On 22 October 1998, Yarra Council circulated a notice that Australand had applied to rezone the convent site for residential use; the application was available for viewing, alongside—as before—a description of the ACC proposal. A new planning scheme amendment, Amendment L83, was drafted to replace the abandoned L54. Soon, nearly 6000 written objections to Amendment L83 had been sent to the City of Yarra.

In November that year, when the ACC and Australand plans were again exhibited at the convent, around 2000 people came. Support for the ACC proposal continued to grow. Yarra Council was not yet 'on side', but it knew the campaign and its supporters couldn't be ignored. Faced with what had become a groundswell of interest in protecting the convent site, it made a strategic exit from the field of battle. In December, it asked the state planning minister to appoint an independent panel and advisory committee that would make recommendations about the site's future use.

In what was now formally a dual planning process (and one that had few precedents), the panel would consider side-by-side the ACC proposal and the principal Australand proposal, then make a recommendation to the council. The final decision would require the approval of the state planning minister.

Now the game was really on. Two contenders had made it to the final race. The battle for the future of the Abbotsford Convent would be hard fought, but on fair terms.

14
Coming and going

A LARGE PART OF life at the Abbotsford Convent revolved around arrivals and departures. New inmates, novices, students, visitors: people were always arriving—and there was an outward flow, too, of graduating students, reformed penitents, mature-age orphans and, occasionally, nuns who had given up their vows.

Of the many additions to and subtractions from the convent population, some were especially dramatic. Infants were left at the convent gates. Inmates broke out by scaling the wall or otherwise escaping. One escape, reported on 9 May 1878 in the *Kilmore Free Press*, the *Portland Guardian* and elsewhere, sheds invaluable light on life at the convent.

Mr and Mrs Moorfield lived across the road from the convent. One morning, Mrs Moorfield was at home alone when she heard a 'hasty knocking'. She opened her door and:

> two females, in what appeared as nuns' habits, rushed into the room, and begged for protection. They stated they had escaped from the convent by climbing over the fence and that they were pursued. In a few moments two other women knocked at the door, and called upon the two refugees by their names, Winifred and Joseph, to come out. This they refused to do, and crouched down into corners, showing great terror, and imploring Mrs Moorfield

not to give them up. Mrs Moorfield was requested to do this by the two persons at the door, and on refusing, she asserts she was threatened with a policeman. This altercation was put an end to by the appearance of the butcher on his morning round, the pursuers then returning to the convent. Tea was then given to the two women, who told Mrs Moorfield that they were 'finally consecrated sisters,' and that they had escaped in the way they had done because there was no other way of getting out. They expressed the utmost terror at the idea of going back, saying they would be severely beaten for having run away. Their dress consisted of black gowns and aprons, a white cloth over the hair, and a black hood. They also wore broad leather belts, with beads and crucifix attached. After staying till about half-past 10 at Mrs Moorfield's, they, very inconsistently with the terror they expressed, went round to the front entrance of the convent to ask for their clothes. They presently returned to Mrs Moorfield's, bringing their clothes with them, as well as 20s. each, which had been given to them by the rev. mother. After exchanging their dresses, they left, telling Mrs Moorfield they were going to St Kilda, where they had friends. This was the last Mrs Moorfield saw of them

Instead of going to St Kilda, however, they went no further than to the house of a Mr Aitkin, who lives close to the convent, and is employed by the institution as a driver of one of the laundry wagons. Mrs Aitkin said the women came to her house at about 11 o'clock on the Friday morning, and that after staying a short time they went into Melbourne, and returned in the evening before dark. On coming back they had 32s. 6d. each, having been to the Nicholson street Convent, where they got 10s. each, and having met Father Quirk, who gave them 2s. 6d. each. Mrs Aitkin, who is a Catholic, and who knows a good deal as to the management of the institution through her husband being employed in it, laughed at the idea of the women being Sisters of the Order of the Good Shepherd, and explained that they were inmates of the Magdalen Asylum, who, because of the length of time they had been there, and their good behaviour, were allowed to wear a habit sufficient to distinguish them from the other Magdalens, or penitents. The two women stayed at Aitkin's cottage all night, still expressing their determination not to return to the asylum. On Saturday morning, another fugitive joined the other two. The story of her escape is very similar to that of the others. The girls appear suddenly to have changed their minds about not returning to their home. Mrs Aitkin stated that Joseph and Winifred first went back. Joseph, being very delicate, was readily re-admitted; Winifred found a little difficulty, but during the afternoon was again received by the rev. mother. The third girl Josephine, did not get back until evening, and then was received reluctantly, as she had given a good deal of trouble previously, and had run away several times before.

Such was the information gleaned outside the convent, and we are bound to say that the prevailing impression on the minds of those who had lived for a few years in the neighbourhood, was that the asylum is rather a prison than a home. The fact that escapes from the Magdalen Reformatory are not infrequent, and that the girls all seek to create sympathy for themselves by much the same story, may account for this impression.

Our representative during the week visited the convent without any previous intimation, and a few minutes after his entrance was favoured with an interview by the Rev. Superioress of the house. On stating the object of his visit, the offer was at once made to take him over each of the institutions within the walls, and to give the minutest information and every facility for the most thorough examination. As regarded the running away, and the return of the three inmates on Friday, the 26th inst., the following particulars were gladly afforded … The two were thus finally consecrated, and the only explanation for leaving the home as they did was that Joseph had had a quarrel with some of the other penitents, during which she received a burn on the neck. That in a freak of ill-temper she determined to leave, but that being too timid to go alone, she got Winifred to go with her. That as they knew there was no hopes of getting permission to go together (for one of the strictest rules of the house is that two penitents shall never be allowed to

> leave together), they walked through the grounds and got over the fence near the river. When they were seen leaving, other penitents were sent after them to induce them to return, but without avail. About an hour after leaving they came to the front gate and asked for their clothes. Those were given to them, also after the usual gratuity of £1 each, though they were not entitled to it, as they had broken the rules of the home. On the following day (Saturday) they again came to the gate, and begged to be allowed to return. With considerable reluctance the rev superioress granted the request, as she feared they had neither friends nor prospects in the world which gave them a hope of a happy life. As regarded the third girl, Josephine, she was young and flighty. Her parents were known, but they refused to take her home, as they had no control over her. She was very troublesome, as she had run away several times, but as leaving her outside was to send her to inevitable ruin, she was always taken back. Such was the plain, impromptu explanation courteously given by the Lady Superior.

A decade later, another escapee ended up in the courts:

> A young girl named Ellen Molony was apprehended yesterday by the Richmond police for having made her escape from the Abbotsford Convent. She sought help from a clergyman at St Ignatius church, Richmond, complaining that 'she was tired of living in the convent' and wanted 'to take a situation'. The police were called and took her into custody. She was later taken back to the convent. At the local police court the next morning, 'Sergeant Bell applied for her discharge, which was granted'.

In 1890, Mary O'Donnell appeared before the Collingwood Magistrates' Court 'in the costume worn by the inmates of the Convent of the Good Shepherd'. She said the Mother Superioress and the nuns were detaining her goods and chattels, and she wished the bench to make an order for their restitution. She had recently been living at Mornington with her husband and two children when her husband, 'in a drunken fit', had threatened to kill her. Afraid for her life, she fled to Hastings to obtain a warrant but returned home to discover her husband and children had left for Melbourne. She followed but could not find them, and 'Being in destitute circumstances, she made application for admission to the Convent of the Good Shepherd.' She was admitted, and remained an inmate for three months, when her 'motherly instincts' reasserted themselves strongly. Longing to see her children, she applied for her release, but was advised to wait a while, as she might change her mind.

> She resolved to escape by scaling the wall ... and making for the police station. Constables Carter and Gleeson were sent to the convent with the woman to verify her story, which proved to be substantially correct, although the Superioress averred that the woman had not been kept against her will, and that it was a rule to tell all women before admitting them that they would be expected to remain for two years. In no case were women kept when they wanted to leave, but for their own good they were persuaded to remain.

O'Donnell's goods and chattels were returned to her but she was unable to find her family. A warrant was issued for her husband's arrest.

The full roll-call of escapees says much about the shape of the convent population, as the following selection shows. In 1911, child-murderer Camelia M'Cluskey forced the lock of her door and absconded but was caught and returned to Abbotsford; in 1915, sixteen-year-old Annie M'Lachlan, small in build and dark in complexion, escaped 'dressed in a striped costume'; and in 1923, a 'rather attractive-looking young girl of 18', originally from the country, induced two companions to escape with her by climbing out on the high roof of the convent, 'riding astride the ridge', and scaling and dropping from two walls, one 12 feet (3.6 metres) high, the other 18 feet (5.5 metres) and 'bristling with broken glass set in cement':

> They avoided injury as much as possible by placing pieces of tin over the glass, and piled empty kerosene tins up against the wall.

> Then they gave each other a leg-up, and dropped to the other side. They were badly shaken and bruised.

In 1927, seventeen-year-old Maisie King escaped with another girl by swimming across the river. She was charged at the Fitzroy Court with vagrancy, but was discharged when the court heard evidence that she had been 'leading a respectable life' and was 'bluffed' into going to the convent, thinking she was being taken to hospital. When the magistrate asked her if she could obtain work, she replied: 'Too right I can.'

In 1929, five girls aged between seventeen and eighteen 'absconded' from the convent after forcing a door. Senior Constable Pattinson, plain-clothes constable Thomas, and constables Henderson and Ryan 'hurried along various streets in Abbotsford, and within five minutes Henderson and Ryan intercepted the girls near the corner of Yarra and Hoddle streets. They were returned to the convent.' Plain-clothes police were again involved in 1930 when an eighteen-year-old girl was injured when she fell from a high wall and struck her head while attempting to escape from the convent one Sunday night: 'The girl disappeared from the casualty ward at the Melbourne Hospital … where she had been taken for treatment.'

15
Implacable

IN FEBRUARY 1999, the state government announced details of the independent panel and advisory committee that would help determine the destiny of the Abbotsford Convent. The state planning minister, Rob Maclellan, appointed three members to the panel: planning expert Kathryn Mitchell, consultant Jeff Lodge and traffic engineer Henry Turnbull. (One of this trio replaced a prior panel member who had to step down after discovering her mother had written a letter of objection to the Australand proposal.) They would investigate Yarra Planning Scheme Amendment L83, Australand's development proposal for the convent site, and the viability of the community's alternative proposal for the site's future use. Over a three-week period, the independent panel would receive submissions, hold public hearings and visit relevant sites. Throughout the hearings, both the Abbotsford Convent Coalition's plans and those of Australand would be on display. In parallel with the panel's investigation, Australand would seek approval from Heritage Victoria for its residential redevelopment; Heritage Victoria's decision on Australand's application was to be presented to the independent panel.

As soon as Yarra Council activated the statutory panel process, the convent campaign shifted into a different gear and on to a different plane. The contest would be fought at a higher level of government, with a greater degree of legal formality and a higher degree of legal peril. To stay in the fight, the ACC would have to navigate a tortuous process with multiple stages, and new costs at every stage. The complex planning rules, for example, required specialist legal, municipal and financial expertise. The panel process, in short, was more than a little daunting. 'We all said, "Oh",' Charlotte Allen recalled. 'We're going to need hefty legal representation.'

Several of the ACC members knew Michelle Quigley via the Public Interest Law Clearing House (PILCH), an independent, not-for-profit legal referral service. Quigley had joined the Victorian Bar in 1988 and was now a prominent barrister, active in planning law and other fields relevant to the convent and the ACC. Through her work at PILCH, she was aware of community campaigns such as those to save Willsmere in Kew and the House of the Gentle Bunyip in Clifton Hill.

Quigley, the ACC members agreed, was the ideal person to have on their side. They approached her and quickly won her over with their proposal. She was generous in her help, offering to devote eight weeks of her time, pro bono, to the hearings process. She led the development of the ACC's panel strategy and tactics, and with her guidance, the ACC members drew up a detailed project plan.

Nigel Lewis brought another key person into the campaign: Patricia O'Donnell. O'Donnell was a major figure in the arts and in the restaurant world. Originally a teacher and educational psychologist, she owned and operated the famous Mietta's Queenscliff Hotel on the Bellarine Peninsula, and, from 1999, North Fitzroy's Star Hotel. A founding donor of the Stella Prize for writing by Australian women, she later turned the Star into a much-loved venue for writers and book launches and book groups.

O'Donnell knew a lot about heritage buildings. She'd bought the Victorian-era Queenscliff Hotel in 1978 with her sisters Robin and Mietta, and Mietta's partner Tony Knox. A major restoration followed. She was also involved in other heritage restoration projects, and knew about the Willsmere campaign.

The ACC also enlisted another major figure: Hilary McPhee. An Abbotsford resident and an early member of the campaign, she was also chair of the Australia Council, Australia's foremost arts body.

In her publishing career, she'd been the first female editor at Penguin Australia before co-founding the famous independent publisher McPhee Gribble.

McPhee agreed to give evidence at the panel hearings, as did her brother, the author and historian Professor Peter McPhee, of the University of Melbourne. Stephanie Alexander also signed on. The ACC was assembling a high-powered team for what threatened to be the most difficult part of the campaign so far.

La Trobe University and the Urban Land Corporation had a barrister on their side, too: a cranky and crusty QC who resembled an old-style litigator from central casting. Thus represented, in March 1999 the two sides geared up for three weeks of hearings at which the panel would scrutinise both proposals. The hearings were held at Richmond Town Hall. The ACC team took notes throughout the hearings and a group of law students from the University of Melbourne assisted. At the end of each day, the campaigners and the students circulated their minutes and notes.

Hilary McPhee, O'Donnell, Peter McPhee and Alexander spoke in favour of the ACC vision, as did Tony and Maureen Wheeler of Lonely Planet. They would happily sign up as tenants, they said. 'Maureen had great presence,' Jo Kinross later recalled. 'Her endorsement was crucial.' Alexander provided advice on the old convent ovens and how they might be used in a cooking school. By appearing at the panel hearings in this way, Alexander and the Wheelers and other witnesses put their reputations on the line for the ACC.

In advance of her appearance, O'Donnell was apprehensive: she didn't particularly enjoy the spotlight, and could see difficulties ahead at the convent site. Many of its larger spaces—the stairwells, the corridors, the balconies—were unlettable. The high-ceilinged spaces, moreover, were difficult to heat, many of the lights were dim, and the acoustics had been designed for whispering and walking, not for commercial letting.

But she knew the importance and potential of the project, and when she appeared in the witness chair she was as emphatic and implacable as granite. She spoke with deep experience and great authority about what was possible and how the project would succeed. Her evidence was crucial.

Throughout the hearings, Quigley's role was equally essential. Kinross sat next to her in the hearings, and the whole time, Kinross later confessed, she was slightly starstruck by the campaign's legal champion. Allen and Margot Foster also recognised the central role that Quigley played.

'Without Michelle's help,' Allen said, 'we would've been crushed.'

'The hearings were very intimidating for a small community group,' Foster said. 'Having Michelle on our side was key.'

• • •

In April 1999, the Heritage Council gave Heritage Victoria an extra thirty days to consider Australand's permit application. The extension followed a request from Heritage Victoria's executive director, Ray Tonkin, who reportedly needed more time to consider an 'extensive internal report' that detailed the 'complicated' implications of Australand's proposal for the multiple registered buildings on the convent site, and the impact on the heritage values of the site as a whole.

Throughout the panel process, the ACC lobbied Heritage Victoria, arguing that the body should refuse to grant Australand a heritage permit for its plans: the site was just too important, and the developer's plans too destructive. In response to Australand's permit application, Heritage Victoria received almost 3000 written objections—an unprecedented number. (According to one rumour, Australand flew a heritage expert down from Queensland to get his advice and perhaps his support, and when he saw what the developer was proposing for the convent site, he told Australand to 'shove it'.)

On 7 May, Heritage Victoria released its answer to Australand's permit application. The heritage body, it seemed, didn't like the Australand proposal. The permit was granted, but with ten pages of stringent and compulsory conditions that would necessitate a total redesign of the residential development plans. From the point of view of heritage compliance, the Australand proposal was history.

Throughout May 1999, the independent panel made a series of site visits that took in Willsmere and the equally vast and handsome former asylum at Caloola in Sunbury. The ACC promoted Caloola, which had been turned into a university campus, as a model of how a low-cost conversion could be achieved at Abbotsford. Several of the consultants who'd worked on the Caloola project assisted the ACC members with their proposal.

At what was a critical stage in the independent panel process, the three panel members visited Mietta's Queenscliff hotel—in part to find a quiet place to deliberate, and in part to see what O'Donnell had been saying about running a viable hospitality business in a restored heritage building. Again O'Donnell was inwardly apprehensive, and again she put on her 'game face'.

'My team rose to the occasion,' she remembered. 'Everything went smoothly.'

Of her heritage building at Queenscliff, O'Donnell said it was 'a work in progress, and always would be'.

Just like the convent.

16
The end of an era

FOR THE GOOD Shepherd's religious community at Abbotsford, the 1960s and 1970s were decades of massive change. In hindsight, they represent the twilight generation of the order's conventual presence on the Abbotsford peninsula. They were decades of transition and, in some cases, demolition.

The 'Juvenile Schools' at Abbotsford and Oakleigh received wards of the state as well as private and 'voluntary' placements. In 1961, the schools were redesignated as 'Youth Training Centres', and the following year, the Magdalen Asylum changed its name to the 'Abbotsford Re-education Home'. More substantial changes would soon follow.

In the 1960s and 1970s, fewer women were choosing to embark on a religious life. The order's population was ageing. Late in the 1960s, it revised its constitution, in part to reflect social changes and the greater liberality within the Church that had been officially endorsed at the Second Vatican Council (1962–65, also called 'Vatican II'). Liturgical changes would be introduced, along with modifications to the sisters' habit and the uniform of novices. In addition, the sisters took specific steps in Australia and New Zealand to streamline and reorganise their order and their work. In a move that would have a significant though temporary impact, they decided to split the Abbotsford Convent into two communities. Broadly speaking, members of one of the communities held more strongly to the order's rules-based past, and members of the other embraced more enthusiastically the new freedoms of the post–Vatican II era. The order engaged the firm of AJ Richardson and Sons to create separate refectories, community rooms and other facilities for the two contiguous communities.

In January 1969, the building rearrangements commenced. According to Catherine Kovesi, 'The only parts of the establishment to be shared by the two new communities were the church, the infirmary and the front entrance. Two lists were posted on the noticeboard—one for sisters who were to form the new "St Peter's Community", and the other for the new "St Paul's Community".' In July that year, the building works were completed.

In May 1970, Mother General Thomas Aquinas (Lee) arrived in Australia 'to make suggestions for the development of [the] Apostolate to suit modern conditions'. As a consequence of those suggestions, an advisory board was established to help manage the order's affairs and assets, and the sisters appointed Malcolm Morrison as lay manager of the laundry (he would resign after just one year in the role).

In July 1971, the order's Provincial Chapter discussed new programs of professional development and new ways to support current and former residents, including through the involvement of lay staff. Sister Bernadette Fox was appointed as the new Mother Provincial and, under the direction of the Mother General, took steps to separate the provincialate from Abbotsford.

On 18 October 1971, the provincialate moved to 6 Thomas Street, Kew. Later that year, the St Joseph's and St Mary's classes were closed. The last of the school-aged children from St Joseph's Class left Abbotsford for the orphanage at St Aidan's in Bendigo, and the spaces for St Mary's Class were repurposed as group rooms for young girls from the new Youth Training Centre. A way of life at Abbotsford was rapidly coming to an end.

Fewer residents meant a requirement for less space and less food. The industrial bakery was suddenly unviable, as were the order's cattle and poultry farms. On 17 October 1972, the sisters sold half of their fine herd of Jersey cows. September 1974 saw another radical step: Abbotsford's laundry business was transferred to Oakleigh. The convent's annalist recorded that momentous decision thus:

> It is now well over one hundred years since the Magdalen Laundry opened its door as a business venture, and during that time it became one of the best known laundries in Melbourne on account of the perfection of its work and the rapidity with which it was done. The whole responsibility for this was borne by the Sisters aided by the women and girls whom they trained to become proficient in all branches of laundry work. Though this work was often pressing, the workers were a happy family who often sang and prayed while they laboured. But during the years changes have gradually taken place in the happy and busy place of work, first all the young girls were withdrawn from the laundry, then gradually some of the older ones. In the meanwhile a male manager was employed with some paid staff and the Sisters were gradually relieved, until today the last four or five were told it was impossible for them to work with the paid staff. It is a sad day for the Sisters, who for so many years, had worked and given of their best for the good of the children whom they were helping to become useful and happy citizens when they return to the world.

The financial burden of maintaining the Abbotsford site was substantial. In 1971, for example, $92,000 was spent on repairs and maintenance. Cleaning the large rooms and long corridors and grand staircases required an ongoing effort of herculean proportions. And despite the ongoing investment in repairs and maintenance, the standard of accommodation was poor, and deteriorating. The fabric of the convent was fraying.

The sisters began to speak of leaving Abbotsford altogether. Such conversations were confronting to some members of the order. Sister Philomene Williams heard someone say, 'Of course the only thing that will have to happen is that Abbotsford will have to go.' Her reaction was emphatic: 'I was just, oh, breathless because Abbotsford had been part of my life all of my life. And I thought: "Oh, how could you say such a thing?"'

Even more radical ideas for change began to take root among the sisters, such as the idea that they should do more work with girls in hostels and within their own families; that they should do more preventive and individualised work such as counselling; that they should care for unmarried mothers through special homes and in smaller units; that there should be specialised programs to combat the effects of alcoholism and drug use; that the sisters should visit women in prison and support them more after their release; that they should provide specialised geriatric care; and, most important of all for the future of Abbotsford, that they should say goodbye to their tradition of institutionalised care.

In 1974 the sisters closed the Abbotsford Youth Training Centre. Later that year, on 22 December, Sister Johanne announced that the Abbotsford Convent would close after 111 summers. The whole of the property, excluding 5 acres (2 hectares), was to be sold. The sisters would retain ownership of the Church of the Immaculate Conception, the Abbotsford Re-education Centre and a small portion of adjacent land; on the latter, they would build a new, smaller convent and an infirmary for elderly nuns and residents. To accommodate the remaining residents, the order would buy houses and units throughout metropolitan Melbourne.

In February 1975, negotiations were completed for the sale of the larger part (36 acres, or 14.5 hectares) of the Abbotsford Convent site to the State College of Victoria for use by its kindergarten training affiliate, the Institute of Early Childhood Development (IECD). The farmland was divided from the main site to establish the Collingwood Children's Farm. The Abbotsford annalist captured in words the sale of most of the convent's land:

> There is no need to mention the sadness that filled the hearts of many of the Sisters of the Province, when they heard the news that Abbotsford had been sold, especially those for whom Abbotsford has been home for the whole of their religious life. However, if they feel much sadness, the older Sisters will ever have the memory of their happy Novitiate days, the joy of

> pronouncing their Vows in the beautiful Convent Chapel, the many ceremonies they had the privilege of assisting at over the years, the enjoyable recreations, especially on feast days when so many made a special effort to be present and add to each other's joy; the happy gatherings on special occasions, when our Sisters from the Foundations joined us, and we could all rejoice together within Abbotsford's spacious rooms. And then there were the days when we worked and recreated with our dear 'children' both young and old, and how many of the latter passed from Abbotsford to their heavenly home.

On 18 September 1975, the *Collingwood Courier* reported that the Lincoln Institute, Victoria's training school for medical therapists, would occupy within three years a large part of the convent site. The sisters ceased to run the convent's schools: from 1976, St Euphrasia's School was to be operated as a parish school and the Commercial School was to be transferred to the IECD.

In May 1976, demolition began of the former home of the St Joseph's Class. The wreckers took 'great care of the slate tiles from the roof, which they said were of superb workmanship and by now very valuable'. By the end of June, the demolition was complete. Three cottages opposite the convent's front entrance were also demolished, along with several farm buildings, the boiler house and the stable.

On 1 July 1976, the keys of Rosina (the former Sacred Heart Class) were handed over to the IECD, and on 20 June 1979, the keys to the old buildings that had housed the Good Shepherd sisters for 116 years were also handed over to the institute. A grand and illustrious antipodean project, launched by four Irish nuns from an obscure European order, had come to an end.

Over the period from 1976 to 1978, the Lincoln Institute of Health Sciences and the Institute of Early Childhood Development established a joint campus on the Abbotsford site. In the following decade, as a result of federal government higher education reforms, the Lincoln Institute became part of La Trobe University and the IECD became part of the University of Melbourne.

At public auctions in 1976 and 1979, the convent's contents were offered for sale. Along with the antique furniture, gates, fittings, religious statues and artworks, there was a fine optometrist's set and a Blüthner grand piano.

17
A gem

AFTER THE DRAMA of the panel hearings, the two sides waited weeks for the decision. When eventually it arrived, on a cold Thursday in June 1999, it was something of an anticlimax.

As part of their program of visits, the members of the independent panel had toured the convent itself and had felt its magic and importance. The members concluded:

> The St Heliers site is a unique place that has a very special place in the history and social and cultural development of Victoria. It is a gem that should not be considered for full residential development as its immediate and only option. Further work should be carried out to pursue the development of the south part of the St Heliers site for an integrated development of the hospitality, arts and cultural purpose.

The panel found that the convent and grounds at the southern end of the site (meaning the larger part, south of St Heliers Street) should remain untouched for two years until other development options had been explored, including cultural tourism opportunities such as a hotel, theatres, restaurants, studios and galleries. A purely residential redevelopment of the southern site was not recommended: 'The convent part of St Heliers should be a site for the people of Victoria.'

The panel endorsed several elements of the Abbotsford Convent Coalition proposal for the southern zone, while some other mooted uses—such as a school, a foundry and a boatbuilding facility—were not supported. It recommended that if after two years no viable alternative and appropriate use could be found, Australand should be allowed to develop the southern part of the site for residential purposes with some limited modifications.

The report called for the state government and the council to take the lead on the future of the precinct. 'The St Heliers site should be seen as a state treasure and resource,' the panel wrote. 'The custodians of the state's interest in this resource need to stand up and be visible, proud and certain.'

The panel didn't block all of Australand's plans. It recommended that the council allow the developer to build intensively on the northern part of the site—the gravelly, weedy area where the first impromptu public meeting had been held, back in 1997. It gave the green light for Australand to construct 100 apartments on the northern zone: specifically, 101 of the originally proposed 239 residential units. This included erecting a nine-storey apartment tower.

Reading the ambiguous findings in the report, both sides were able to claim victory. It was certainly a partial victory for the ACC: the independent panel had recognised the Abbotsford Convent's heritage and cultural values. Margot Foster said the findings also endorsed the ACC's plan to protect the main convent building and grounds as a public precinct. And they were a major setback, she said, for the developer: 'Australand's plans are now in shreds. Their proposal to convert the heritage-listed buildings has been rejected, as has their plan to build new apartment blocks among the heritage buildings.'

A representative of the ULC also spoke positively of the panel's report, but Australand was naturally unhappy with the ambivalent recommendation and the possibility of a two-year delay. 'We've already been through a long and exhaustive consultative process,' Australand manager Robert Pradolin told a journalist. 'We would've preferred the panel to make the hard decisions now.'

• • •

Up to this point, Yarra Council had played its cards close to its chest. The ACC didn't know where Yarra stood. Now, in light of the independent panel findings, the council held talks with the ACC, Australand, the Urban Land Corporation, La Trobe University and the state government. It considered the advisory committee's report and then readied itself to make a final decision about the Australand proposal.

Around the same time, in August 1999, the ACC held a public meeting at Collingwood Town Hall. More than 700 people attended, including Yarra councillors. The celebrity speaker was Cr Dick Gross, author and mayor of the City of Port Phillip. The meeting affirmed emphatic support for the ACC proposal. Afterwards, Yarra Council met and resolved to abandon Planning Amendment L83. The Australand application lapsed, and the council made detailed recommendations to develop an alternative use for the convent site along the lines of the ACC proposal.

Soon after, the council organised a public meeting on St Heliers Street, complete with brass band and marquee. Hundreds of people were there when Mayor Steve Watson made a big announcement: the City of Yarra was abandoning the planning amendment and rejecting the developer's second planning application. Yarra had come over to the ACC's side. At this landmark moment—the first time the campaigners knew they had local government backing—the heavens opened and everyone was drenched.

The ACC would soon have other powerful supporters. In a 1998 by-election, former ABC journalist and presenter Mary Delahunty had been elected to the Victorian Legislative Assembly seat of Northcote. If the government changed at the forthcoming state election, there was a good chance that she would be arts minister. Jo Kinross knew her, as did Bill Russell through Jock Rankin, who was Delahunty's husband and the head of the Property Council in Victoria.

Delahunty had added some words to Labor's election platform to the effect that, if elected, a state Labor government would turn the convent into an arts and education precinct. The commitment was subject to a solid business case being prepared for the project.

In September 1999, the state election was held. After a strong protest vote and a stinging repudiation of attacks on public institutions such as the auditor-general and the ABC—the Kennett Government had planned to privatise parts of the audit office, and Jeff Kennett himself infamously threw a spadeful of sand at an ABC camera crew—the government unexpectedly changed from Liberal to Labor, and the new state premier was Steve Bracks.

In the aftermath of this surprise result, Yarra Council approached the state government with a suggestion: there might be a way to determine the viability of the ACC proposal and solve the issue of the convent's future once and for all. The council proposed that a working party, with suitably broad representation, should nut out a way forward.

Through November and December 1999, Yarra Council and the new state government worked on the governance and functions of the working party that would consider the future of the site. The working party's structure and terms of reference were assembled and agreed in principle: it would be a Project Facilitation Reference Group (PFRG) and would investigate uses of the site—for arts, education and tourism—with a view to reporting back in November 2000. (This was an agonisingly long timeline, and some in the campaign saw the PFRG process as an attempt by the government to avoid making a decision about the site.) Upon receiving the report, the planning minister would decide either to ratify Yarra Council's decision to reject the residential proposal, or to approve Australand's application for rezoning the site as land for residential development.

Early in 2000, the PFRG was convened. Richard Wynne, still the local member for the seat of Richmond (which includes Abbotsford), arranged for Rob Adams of the City of Melbourne to chair the group. Its other members included representatives from the state government (Alex Lawlor from Arts Victoria, Peter McEwan from the Department of Infrastructure, and Matt Faubel from the ULC), Yarra Council, Australand (Rob Pradolin) and the ACC (Kinross and Tony Lee).

In support of the PFRG's deliberations, economist Marcus Spiller did some groundbreaking work on the evaluation of the convent site. In seeking to find the value of the site at its 'highest and best use', he noted that in an urban environment, open space is worth a lot. Spiller attempted to measure that worth, and used his estimate to prove that the value of the convent site would be higher as a community asset and as an area of open space than as a closed residential development.

In November 2000, the PFRG finalised its report and presented it to the minister for planning, John Thwaites. The state government considered the report and prepared a response. The ACC put up a new batch of billboards and posters, this time asking when the government would finally step up for Abbotsford. One simple but striking poster had just three lines, in large letters:

> Heritage support: Tick.
> Local government support: Tick.
> State government support: ?

It was a big question mark.

18
Everything you wanted

THE OUTCOME OF the PFRG process was essentially the same as the ambivalent result of the independent panel hearings: the arts precinct proposal was a great idea, but financially it might not work. And the ACC members had their own big question mark—over the viability of their proposal.

Despite this ambiguous landing point, the PFRG process did yield dividends for the 'save' campaign. It enabled the ACC to spread the word and engage more widely about the alternative proposal. Critically, many more people inside the government and the state bureaucracy were exposed to the ACC option.

The PFRG process also allowed the ACC to augment its case with more concrete information, such as market research on how people would actually use a community-owned convent site. But the government still wasn't prepared to back the ACC solution. So, once again, the campaigners reached out to their supporters within the public sector and the parliament. Jo Kinross and Sally Romanes spoke to Mary Delahunty, who continued to advocate within the government for the community proposal. Richard Wynne, now parliamentary secretary to the premier, was also vocal in his support, as was planning minister John Thwaites, who had been convinced of the merits of the community solution.

Some ministers and officials in the Bracks Government had dug in their heels in opposition to the ACC vision, but Premier Steve Bracks himself was increasingly in favour. His wife, Terry, had already seen the site and been won over, and the head of the Department of Premier and Cabinet (DPC), Terry Moran, was also coming round. When Moran saw aerial photos, he was struck by the precinct's beauty and importance. The captivating, mind-changing power of the site was strong enough, it seemed, to persuade even the most sceptical senior bureaucrats.

Rob Adams met with Minister Thwaites to deliver a verbal account of the PFRG's work. The project could be viable, he said, if the redevelopment and refurbishment of the southern site proceeded in stages. On 20 December 2000, Thwaites told a local newspaper he'd not yet made a decision on the site but was reviewing the PFRG report and the convent site had significant heritage value that needed to be protected.

The process stretched on for another six agonising months. Behind the formal discussions there were a lot of informal conversations and machinations. People were in the premier's ear about the site—people such as Lady Southey, former Deputy Prime Minister and Uniting Church minister Brian Howe, and state Labor politician and architect Evan Walker. State bureaucrats were also coming up with different options, such as the possibility of granting a limited twenty-year lease. MPs rejected that option as unviable. For the site to work as a community-owned arts precinct, it needed long-term security so it could find secure, long-term tenants.

All the different discussions came to a head at a key meeting in Premier Bracks' office. MPs Wynne and Rob Hudson were both there when the premier said, 'We will do this. We will fund it, but on the condition that it is viable and you won't be coming back for money.'

On 12 June 2001, the Bracks Government announced it had approved the proposal for a cultural precinct on the southern site. It was entrusting the future of the Abbotsford Convent to the community. A grant of $4 million from the Community Support Fund was approved to help establish the site as a viable arts, education and cultural precinct, 'as a gift from this generation of Victorians to our children and grandchildren'.

Within the government, Delahunty, along with Wynne and Hudson, had been instrumental in the decision. The announcement was of course wonderful news for the ACC and their supporters, but it had big strings attached. The handover was conditional on the government receiving and approving an acceptable site master plan and an acceptable business case. According to the formal deed that would eventually set out the terms of the transfer of the site, the community solution had to be financially sustainable: otherwise, the site would revert to the government.

Members of the ACC perceived this clause in multiple ways. Some saw it as a clever way for the government to placate naysayers inside the state bureaucracy. Others saw it as a means by those naysayers to open up a window of exit, a way out of the handover, and also a way to reduce the extent to which the ACC's victory in the 'save' campaign could serve as a precedent for other heritage assets. More than one person saw the conditions as an attempt to insert a 'poison pill' into the deed. Patricia O'Donnell said, 'The deed was written with the expectation that the convent project would fail and the site would be returned as a "failed community campaign".'

The conditions for handing the site back to the state were easy to trigger. They felt to some like a 'Sword of Damocles' over the site and the project. Under the deed, even approaching the government to seek more money would be counted as an 'act of default'. Perversely, though, the hair-triggers in the deed made everyone in the campaign more determined than ever to make the community model work.

In another sense, too, there were poisons involved. Charlotte Allen was one of the ACC members who saw that the southern site alone—without the northern car park—was unworkable, a poisoned chalice. One campaigner said the convent without a car park would be like a car with three wheels. The PFRG had found that the northern section of the convent site should be used for low-rise commercial and residential development. To the consternation of Yarra Council and the community, the state government had agreed, promising the northern site to Australand for an 'approved development' of nine to twelve storeys.

Hard upon the state government's decision to transfer the southern site to the community, Wynne called Kinross to share the happy moment. 'I've given you everything you wanted,' he said.

'No you haven't,' Kinross replied. 'We need the northern site. The project won't work without it.'

19
Saved

'IN A PART of Melbourne not well served by public transport,' Charlotte Allen said, 'the community precinct and the farm could never work without parking.'

Amanda Stone, Margot Foster and Jo Kinross agreed. Under the state government's split north–south solution, both the Children's Farm and the convent would effectively have no parking. Under that scenario, neither could be viable. The car park was essential for access and for financial sustainability.

Thus began the 'Battle for the Car Park'. At the high point of hostilities, under the banner of 'taking the farm to the city', the campaigners filled a trailer with dogs and a herd of the Children's Farm goats and took them to Spring Street. Melbourne's television news bulletins featured the goats—and the pungent messages they left behind—on the steps of Parliament House. As the animals circled and bleated and pooed, Premier Steve Bracks and Parliamentary Secretary Richard Wynne looked on from their offices inside.

At various stages in the campaign, the ACC had accepted or entertained plans for a high-rise development on the northern site—perhaps as a trade-off for saving the southern site, or as a way to fund its preservation. Therefore, in all good conscience the ACC couldn't now oppose Australand's plans for the northern site. The residents formed a new group—the Collingwood and Abbotsford Residents

Association—to continue the fight, and to champion the argument that the car-park land had belonged all along to the community.

The residents also bought some insurance by obtaining a legal covenant over the car-park land, and a caveat on the title of the whole convent site. The goal was to prevent secret transfers and other covert dealing. With these protections in place, the government and the Urban Land Corporation couldn't transfer the title without telling the residents.

• • •

In addition to the battle for the car park, the battle for the main southern site continued.

It wasn't enough that the ACC had convinced the community and Yarra Council of the merits of the alternative, community-driven solution. Nor was it enough that major philanthropists had pledged their support, or that paying tenants were queuing up to use the convent spaces, or that the independent panel and the PFRG had endorsed the heritage values of the site and the merits of an arts and education solution. The government wanted to see a quantitative, financial, rock-solid, rolled-gold, bulletproof business case.

It also wanted to see the fine print of how the site would be governed and managed. What kind of entity would oversee and steer the convent once it passed into community ownership?

That part was relatively straightforward. With the help of lawyers from Freehills, the Abbotsford Convent Implementation Group (ACIG)—formed in July 2001 under the chairmanship of Noel Henderson, a senior executive with international construction firm Multiplex—drew up board charters and other foundational documents. The convent, in public hands, would be owned and run by a community body, the Abbotsford Convent Foundation (ACF), whose members would own the site on behalf of all Victorians. The ACF would have charitable status, which meant gifts and donations would be tax deductible. Bill Russell and Sally Romanes were the founding office bearers, serving as chair and deputy chair respectively.

Finalising the business case was more difficult. The handover condition was that an acceptable master plan and business case would be submitted to the government. The ACIG was tasked with developing these, with the aim that they would be enough to trigger the government's support.

A big effort was put into preparing the business case. Yarra Council contributed around $1 million to the process. People with relevant expertise and experience were drafted in, including Patricia O'Donnell, Russell, Andrea Hull (former head of the Victorian College of the Arts), Roger Allen (of well-known Sydney-based venture capitalists Allen & Buckeridge), Mike Smith (former editor of *The Age*), Hayden Raysmith (founding chair of the Melbourne Community Foundation) and, from the ACC, Kinross, Romanes and Tony Lee (focusing on the heritage and architectural sides of the group's work).

As with the first ACC committees, each member of the ACIG brought crucial skills and capabilities. Hull, for example, had a strong background and network in the arts sector. Raysmith was an astute thinker and advocate who'd had a lot of experience in community campaigns and activism; he also had excellent government relationships. State MP Rob Hudson had asked Raysmith to bring into the ACIG process people who would add further heft. Raysmith brought in Allen, who in turn knew the consultants Booz Allen. Kate McCaughey was seconded from the City of Yarra to act as the ACIG's executive officer, and Allen had a property in Fitzroy that he lent to the group to use as its office.

After Henderson stepped down from the ACIG, Russell acted as chair. The group members developed costings and tested the validity of the ACC solution. They navigated a lengthy process with the state government in which senior officials and bureaucrats tested every input and assumption and output of the business case. One question was key: what would be the actual cost of repurposing the convent buildings?

That cost depended in a direct way on the standard of restoration and refurbishment. Nigel Lewis agreed with Henderson and Russell that the convent buildings didn't need to be restored to a shiny commercial standard. In fact, that was a terrible idea as it would obscure the layers of heritage and signs of previous use that the ACC and the community were intent on protecting. On that basis, the business planning process showed that the alternative solution could work.

The convent campaign had begun in a suburban car park and around a suburban kitchen table. Now, the implementation group process brought together some of the biggest corporate names in Melbourne: architects, builders, law firms, property agents, consultants. Multiplex, PricewaterhouseCoopers, Allens, Freehills, Rider Hunt, Denton Corker Marshall, Colliers. All these names provided input into the ACIG process and into the business case and master plan. Russell saw this as crucial. 'It showed that the "top end of town" was behind the project,' he said. 'And it meant the government couldn't fault the document.'

In February 2002, the Abbotsford Convent Foundation delivered to the state government the business case and master plan, together with financial pledges totalling $3 million. The documents provided for a phased five-year $10 million program to bring the convent precinct into full operation as a community asset.

• • •

In the end, the moment the ACC members had dreamed about—the handing-over of the keys to the convent—was a low-key affair. At around 4 p.m. on 27 April 2004, Peter Carroll and Geoff Mills of the Treasury Department's property group telephoned Russell. Soon they were at his office with a photographer in tow, handing over the keys and the title to the southern part of the site. 'The government had run out of questions,' Russell said. 'They'd finally satisfied themselves that we did have a sustainable business case.'

That evening, Russell went home, picked up his wife and teenage children, and took them to the convent. Night had fallen and the Russells were carrying torches. They unlocked the gate and entered the dark, forbidding, derelict site. In the main convent buildings, windows were boarded up, glass was cracked and tiles were chipped and broken. Some doors were hanging off their hinges, others lay on the ground. The buildings were overgrown with creepers, the grounds with weeds and bracken. A dominant thought was in Russell's mind: *How are we going to make this work?*

Despite the veneer of dilapidation, the buildings had strong bones. 'They'd been built to last,' Russell said. To help kick off the restoration works, the state government handed over the $4 million from the Community Support Fund, and the City of Yarra provided $1 million.

As Russell later reflected, there was a lot to be done to ready the site for opening: 'Now that we had the title, we had a few things to do. We needed to get the buildings secure from the weather and the wildlife. We had to upgrade the services, the fire mains, the gas supply (some of these were unexpected). We needed to remove all the asbestos. We had to lock in tenants, such as the Steiner School, 3MBS and the Bakery (we needed the revenue). We had to get building and planning permits so we could occupy the buildings. We needed staff and an organisational structure. We needed to harness our volunteers (how wonderful were they then, as now). We needed to work within our budget, self-funded and without borrowings. We needed to work with the Children's Farm, the council and other stakeholders. We needed to get more funding from philanthropists and grant bodies and other contributors. And we needed to consolidate public support for what we were trying to achieve.'

The ACF set up a building committee that reported to the board and met at least once a week to oversee the restoration of the buildings and infrastructure. It had a broad representation, including state government, the council and volunteers.

Three staff were appointed. As general manager, Geoff Day did a thousand essential and practical things to prepare the southern site for opening. He shooed away the pigeons and possums and bats. He cleared away the ivy, the blackberries, the brambles and the moss. He got tenants into the lettable spaces, and oversaw restoration of parts of the Providence Building so that the ACF, too, would have a home. There was lots of work on walls and floors and ceilings and pipes.

As the scale of the task became clearer, the cost of readying the site began to rise. With funding from the federal government, a 'Green

Corps' team of ten young people and a supervisor helped clear out the gardens. 'For months they worked to get rid of the blackberries and ivy,' Charlotte Allen remembered. 'They uncovered the pergola, which had disappeared, and the brick road at the bottom of the gardens and all the pathways.'

In early May 2004, within the first two weeks of receiving the southern title, the ACF hosted an open day that attracted more than 4500 people. To many of those, it was another very emotional occasion.

On the Friday before the open day, Russell and Day and some other convent people worked well into the night to make sure the commercial kitchen would be ready. 'The gas was only connected about 4 p.m.,' Russell said. 'It was very tight but it ended up a great weekend with thousands of people coming through. It was an exciting time.'

On the eve of the public opening, the ACC members gathered for a picnic in the rotunda. They had the whole site to themselves. And now, on behalf of and as members of the community, they owned it. They wandered around, exploring the gardens and the buildings. It was wonderful to be there at that moment, victorious in the campaign. And it was a remarkably odd feeling being there alone, having the site to themselves, knowing it would never be like this again.

Kinross expressed the strangeness of the moment: 'It felt unbelievable on one level but totally normal and inevitable on another.'

The critical site works continued apace until, on 1 May 2005, a year after restoration started, the convent's gates were permanently opened to the public. The site had had an official opening as a religious community in 1863. Now it was being opened again, this time as a community-owned arts and cultural precinct.

Hilary Rankin called it a historic day. And she was right.

• • •

Without the northern site, there was still the problem of car parking. One option was to use parkland on the northern side of Johnston Street and at the bottom of Clarke Street—but the loss of parkland was undesirable, and would never be acceptable to the community.

The ACF urgently needed the northern site, which the state government had promised to Australand.

'There was a high degree of difficulty with the northern site,' Steve Bracks later said. 'We had to think about sovereign risk. Australand had clear rights and approval to go ahead. We could only go ahead if we had Australand's cooperation.'

Russell knew Rob Pradolin well. He sought and was granted permission at the next ACF board meeting to go to see Pradolin with Day. Russell told Pradolin there was strong community opposition to Australand's plans for the northern site. Pradolin could live with the expected level of opposition, he said. It was 'a normal part of the development game'. But he had always recognised that the car park would be vital to the ongoing viability of the convent and the farm. Knowing that, he had held off lodging a planning application with the City of Yarra for the northern site.

What Pradolin said next was a turning point. He undertook to propose to the Australand Board that they relinquish their right to develop the car-park site, as long as someone covered the costs the developer had incurred to date—something like $1.4 million. 'The car park had to remain a car park,' Pradolin later said. Relinquishing the site was a surprising decision for a developer. But it was, he said, the right thing to do.

Russell reported back to the ACF board. The quantum of money was substantial, but there was optimism among the board members. 'We will get it,' Romanes said.

The financial news, though, was about to get much worse. Australand may have been prepared to walk away for $1.4 million, but the ULC wanted more than ten times that amount. The ACF and its supporters might be able to find a million or two, but scraping together $17 million to cover the ULC's costs was out of the question.

Throughout this period, Wynne was very active in trying to find a way forward. He phoned Russell every week and chased down all sorts of potential solutions, such as possible land offsets—like vacant school sites—that could be offered to the ULC. Hudson, too, continued to push the community's case, as did Mary Delahunty, though she was pessimistic about finding any more money for the campaigners and their proposal.

Local residents continued to prosecute the argument for the northern site to be retained as car parking for the convent and the Children's Farm. Kinross, Stone and the Collingwood and Abbotsford Residents Association were at the forefront of this campaign.

Russell continued to meet behind the scenes with the government and its central agencies of DPC and Treasury. As the discussions became more detailed, Treasury started bringing lawyers from Clayton Utz to the meetings. Over a weekend, Russell and Day wrote up a prospective memorandum setting out how the convent and the Children's Farm could share the car spaces and the revenue from the car park. They initially proposed allocating ten spaces, and 20 per cent of the car-park revenue, to the farm. The Treasury officials came back with a counter-proposal of twelve spaces for the farm, and Russell quickly agreed: 'The only change they made to our draft memorandum was to increase by two the number of parking spots we gave the farm. I didn't argue.' The officials went off to seek senior ministers' approval. Verbal approval was forthcoming, and Wynne came in person to advise the ACF at its next board meeting.

Eight years after the previous government had slated the convent site for apartments, the Bracks Government recognised that parking was crucial to the precinct's success. Australand had agreed to withdraw, and the government had agreed to sort out the ULC's $17 million hole. The ACF now owned the northern site. The ACC and its allies had won the battle to protect the convent site in its entirety.

That night, on 8 July 2005, the campaigners held a celebratory dinner. The convent was complete and it could now thrive. 'We did it,' Charlotte Allen later reflected, 'and we couldn't believe it.'

That same night, Russell stepped down as chair of the ACF—his work was done. 'I was overwhelmed,' he said, 'but very pleased.'

Raysmith became the foundation's new chair. The following Saturday, an event was held to formally hand over the northern site's title to the community. On the way there, Raysmith was in the car with Premier Bracks when the premier told him at the last minute that the government would stump up the $1.4 million. The ACF was off the hook for that amount as well.

At the event, Russell received the northern title from the premier, and Wynne spoke of the significance of the moment: 'This is the missing piece of the puzzle in the St Heliers convent precinct that the community has fought hard and long for.'

Bracks spoke, too. He described it as a proud moment: 'The unique rural setting of the convent and the Children's Farm, so close to the centre of Melbourne, is an important asset, not only for the local community but for all Victorians.'

Allen, newly appointed as deputy chair of the ACF, was optimistic about the future of the site. 'There is every sign that this is going to be a real winner for everybody,' she said. 'Given the past eight years, it is hard not to be hopeful.'

Australand manager Rob Pradolin reportedly felt mixed emotions about ending the company's eight-year association with the site. (During the campaign, he had arrived at a personal vision not too dissimilar to that of the campaigners. The main difference was that he envisaged people living on site, above the ground floor, thereby providing passive security and a revenue stream from annual owner fees to maintain the heritage buildings.) But Frank Palomares, acting manager of the Children's Farm, was delighted: 'This means the future of the farm is secure, and we can grow and prosper.' (The Collingwood Children's Farm is now the oldest working farm on freehold land in Victoria.)

O'Donnell called the convent campaign 'a victory for the people of Melbourne', one that was achieved 'through sheer grit and determination'.

For Kinross, the moment was especially satisfying. After years of setbacks and small victories, she could finally rejoice. 'The various celebrations up to this point have always felt a bit premature, but now we can all truly celebrate a victory,' she said. 'There aren't too many good-news stories of this kind around anymore.'

Premier Bracks called in at a new establishment upstairs in the main convent building. 'Handsome Steve's House of Refreshment' was a tiny terrazzo-floored bar–cafe crammed with Geelong Football Club memorabilia. Bracks was (and remains) a one-eyed Geelong supporter. Sometimes at Handsome Steve's there was naked dancing on tables; sometimes there were fights and other chaotic scenes. Today, however, there was just a general feeling of relief and joy and goodwill.

20
Open

AT THE TIME of the first Australand proposal, there was very little high-rise development along the Yarra outside the CBD, and there were large areas of vacant and underdeveloped land nearby, such as in East Richmond. Today, however, public open space is at a premium, the Yarra is at risk of encroachment and overshadowing as never before, and the density and desirability of suburbs like Richmond and Abbotsford have skyrocketed. In retrospect, the decision to protect the convent site from intensive redevelopment looks extremely wise.

From an early stage, the ACC members' campaign to save the convent had three threads: they were running a grassroots community campaign; they were formal participants in a protracted, complex and precedent-setting municipal planning process; and they were social entrepreneurs developing a multimillion-dollar project for an alternative use that met the needs of the site and the community and would be acceptable to government.

Looking back on the campaign, its leaders see a tableau of almost mythical moments. The first car-park meeting. Sue's kitchen. The Steiner School classroom. The crowded senior citizens' room at the Collingwood Town Hall. The drenching rain at the marquee event. The open days. The panel hearings. The final handover of the whole site. The campaign's big victory, built as it was on a drawn-out series of small wins. At several points, the campaigners felt they had just scraped through by the skin of their teeth. But Nigel Lewis knew the ACC had pulled off something spectacular: 'the longest-running and most professional and successful heritage campaign in Australia'.

Through the late 1990s and early 2000s, the campaigners devoted much of their lives to securing the convent for the community. It was a fight for what one writer at *The Age* called a 'heritage headache'.

For Jo Kinross, the campaign was an all-consuming project. She and her husband, David, did not see the grain of their kitchen table for eight years. In a surprising way, it was the ideal project for Kinross: it used every part of her character and every line of her CV. Her experiences in counselling, community development, public policy, education, wellness and advocacy were all brought to bear, including in the positivity of the ACC's approach.

'Jo didn't allow conflict within the group or in the campaign,' Tony Lee remembers.

'We avoided getting into "opposite corners",' Kinross says. 'Even with the Australand people we would always share a respectful smile, even at the toughest stages in the planning process.'

After the convent reopened in its new incarnation as a community arts precinct, Kinross made a visit and was struck by what she saw. The site was busy with people shopping at the 'shirt and skirt' market, visiting the vegetarian restaurant and enjoying the grounds. 'It was exactly what I'd seen in my mind's eye,' she said.

Having that concrete vision in view—and sticking to it—was crucial. As people came and went in the campaign, and as daily issues popped up and were resolved, Kinross kept her eye—and the energy of the campaign—focused on the vision. Bill Russell puts it this way: 'We achieved something no one thought we could. It was thanks to the many people who contributed to this amazing chapter of the convent.'

Hilary Rankin has done a stocktake of people who were active in the Abbotsford Convent campaign. There were actors, comedians, musicians, farmers, gardeners, teachers, carpenters, lawyers, architects, schoolchildren, university students, trade unionists, boatbuilders, graphic artists, psychologists, healers, broadcasters, journalists, psychiatrists, real estate agents, weavers, businesspeople, painters, sculptors, librarians, writers, accountants, philanthropists, ceramicists, curators, researchers, historians, footballers, social workers, plumbers, academics, electricians, photographers, drivers, doctors, carers, jewellers, nuns, judges, retirees, IT workers, politicians, retailers, hoteliers, restaurant owners. Plus councillors from the cities of Yarra, Boroondara and Port Phillip. The ACC was made up of people from all sectors and all walks of life.

From the beginning, the ACC's approach was rigorous and strategic. Plans were made, minutes were kept, tasks were delegated, and the campaign built a network of expert helpers as well as the influencers from the 'Great and the Good' list. The commitment of the core ACC members was unwavering, and decisive.

Sally Romanes sees several ingredients in the campaign's success: 'Grind, grit, determination. The ability to look after each other. Differentiation of tasks. Being very task-focused, but never forgetting the end goal. Celebrating the milestones. Keeping up energy levels. I remember Jo was brilliant at this. If someone couldn't contribute at that point then another person could take the lead. Jo used the analogy of a skein of geese: the leader of the V does the most work and the geese behind get the benefit of the slipstream. When the leader tires, another member of the skein takes up the leading edge.'

For the campaigners and the first members of the ACF, the convent was a family affair. 'It was fantastic,' Russell says, 'to see how we all got our family and friends involved. It was not just the board and committee members but all their families and friends who volunteered. My wife and children thought I was just about living at the convent, as were many of the board members.'

The early decision of the ACC to adopt a nonpartisan approach and to cultivate support from all major political parties was a smart move. So was the early shift from an oppositional campaign to putting forward a positive alternative. That shift, which switched the campaign's energy at a formative stage from negative to positive, was crucial for the motivation and wellbeing of the campaigners.

Most community groups implode because of personality conflicts. Most campaigns fail. The ACC successfully coordinated the efforts of thousands of people over eight years. The ethos of openness was vital, as was the positive approach and the willingness to let go. Handing over the site to the ACF was one of many key turning points in the campaign. To their credit, the ACC members and other residents and campaigners didn't hold on too long to the site or the fight. They were ready to step back without rancour, and to hand over the asset and the project to a new set of stewards, while continuing to advise and guide.

'They were low-ego people,' Charlotte Allen says. 'They always knew that at some point there would be a pivot to another phase.'

'The board dynamic was very important,' Mike Smith says. 'The members were passionate but also cohesive and respectful of the chair and each other. It was so important in what were sometimes fractious times outside to have a solid and cohesive board.'

Above all, the magic and significance of the site won the day. Looking back, Steve Bracks described the Abbotsford peninsula as 'a historic site, a strategic site, and now a focus for the community. It would have been a tragedy to privatise this stretch of the Yarra river.'

'It was the site that was always going to win,' Lewis says. 'You just had to get people down there to recognise its value. Once people realised the value of the site, we felt quietly confident.' Russell agrees: 'The convent just should never have been viewed as a residential development site.'

'This wasn't just another battle against inappropriate development,' Kinross says. 'The power and special values of the site itself were critical factors.'

Richard Wynne, still the local member and now the state planning minister, sees the victory as without precedent in Australia. The convent site had effectively been sold to a developer. On the northern site in particular, Australand had both legal ownership of the land and planning approval for an apartment building. To overturn that sale was an ambitious ask, Minister Wynne says. But Australand and Rob Pradolin, to their credit, were prepared to concede the northern and southern sites, at cost and without taking the matter to court or otherwise seeking restitution or compensation for the lost development potential.

• • •

The new convent enterprise needed a new CEO. Global headhunters Egon Zehnder agreed to conduct the search pro bono. In the firm's Melbourne office, Neil Waters presented the ACF board with a short list of people who might be described as 'safe' candidates. 'And then there's Maggie,' he added, almost apologetically. 'You might want to interview her, too.'

Maggie Maguire had been working at the state government arts body, Arts Victoria. At the appointed interview time, she arrived with purple hair and a compelling CV. Patricia O'Donnell saw that Maggie had previously run a business and worked at the coalface in the arts sector. This was the combination the convent needed. The board's decision was immediate and unanimous. 'There was no question that Maggie was the one,' Allen later said.

In 2006, Maguire was appointed as the Abbotsford Convent's first CEO. O'Donnell feared that once Maguire fully apprehended the scale of the task before her, she would 'run screaming from the project'. But she didn't. Working closely with Hayden Raysmith and the other directors, she proved to be a strong, creative and entrepreneurial CEO. She and her team shouldered a massive workload with little backup.

Maguire tells astounding stories of her first days at the convent. Adventures with unruly visitors and tenants. Disasters with plumbing and ceilings. The delight of seeing layers of modern paint and varnish removed to reveal beautiful heritage tilework and timberwork. Dealing with threshold decisions and practical heritage questions, like whether to paint the steel columns in the cloister.

The language in the convent deed about being 'self-supporting' echoed what the sisters first said in 1863. The challenge now confronting Maguire and her team was the same one that had confronted the nuns at the site: how to make it viable. In the foundational years of the ACF, there was a constant fear of financial ruin. 'Things kept breaking and blowing up,' Maguire said. 'The more people came to the site, the more things needed to be repaired or replaced.'

There was much learning about the physical management of people who were enjoying and moving through the convent precinct. In the early days there was no venue hire business but there were impromptu events, such as an informal concert that attracted hundreds of people to listen to Nigel Kennedy play violin. The convent would get better at hosting events like this and ultimately become a treasured destination for music and theatre and other performances.

The convent project had shifted gears several times, and now Maguire oversaw another phase shift: from the community campaign and the planning project to the daily reality of being a landlord. In that role, there was again a lot of 'learning by doing' for the convent's leaders. How to select and manage tenants. How to make sure that, once selected, the tenants paid the rent. 'There was no rulebook or guidebook for what we were doing,' Maguire said. Finding more tenants and hosting more events would be critical to making the community model work. 'We wanted people who had a vision.'

In 2006, the first major commercial tenants commenced trading, including the Convent Bakery and Lentil as Anything restaurant. The Sophia Mundi Steiner School moved its primary school to the newly restored St Mary's Building. Other foundational tenants included the Northern Melbourne Institute of TAFE and 3MBS classical radio. In recognition of the site's Indigenous history and significance, the Wurundjeri Woi Wurrung Cultural Heritage Aboriginal Corporation established its first headquarters there.

Corporate governance was another zone of learning. In the early days, the ACF board functioned more like a committee of management than a proper corporate board. The individual board members had their own keys to the site and were deeply involved in day-to-day operational issues, such as staffing and tenancy. Gradually, though, it began to function more like a governing board and the ACF adopted a more conventional division of roles between board and management.

With care and vigour, Maguire steered the Abbotsford Convent through its infancy and into adulthood. Supported by an indefatigable chief operating officer, John Di Natale, she built a strong and flexible management team to manage the convent's buildings, tenancies, events and fundraising.

'Maggie was fantastic for the convent,' Russell says.

'It could never have been done without Maggie,' said O'Donnell. 'She was extraordinarily resilient. It was her resilience and stamina that saw us through.'

Maguire's decade as convent CEO ended in 2016, and the ACF board embarked on a process to find and appoint a new head. There was a strong field: the role had become desirable and sought-after, which said a lot about how far the convent had come, and a lot about Maguire's achievements. It also spoke volumes about the potential of a site that had become extremely important to Melburnians, a landmark in the same category as the Melbourne Zoo or the Royal Botanic Gardens.

In September 2016, the ACF board appointed Collette Brennan as the new CEO. Brennan brought a strong background in the performing arts, youth arts and public programming. Her CV included several senior roles with the Australia Council for the Arts, executive director of Circa Contemporary Circus, and founding creative director of The Edge, the State Library of Queensland's program for children and young people.

Brennan's vision for the convent includes widening the range of arts and cultural events and activities there; deepening connections with other monastic and heritage sites in Australia and abroad; advancing the restoration and activation of major buildings; and continuing to build the inspiring community of artists, cultural organisations, wellbeing practitioners, educators and broadcasters who are the site's heart and soul.

• • •

On 31 August 2017, the Abbotsford Convent was added to the Australian National Heritage List. This acknowledgement—Australia's highest level of heritage recognition—placed it alongside such landmarks as the Royal Exhibition Building, the Sydney Opera House and the Melbourne Cricket Ground.

The Abbotsford Convent became the model for how to revive and repurpose an asset for the community. Other projects from around the world—former convents, railway stations, gaols, hospitals—now look to it for lessons and insights.

After more than twenty years, the campaigners still meet from time to time. The 'Separation' oak tree, said to have been planted by Edward Curr, still stands in the convent grounds. Possums and bluetongues still occupy parts of the site. And the clock of the Church of the Immaculate Conception still keeps time.

After leading the ACC's involvement in the panel hearings, Michelle Quigley became a senior counsel, and in 2017 she was appointed to Victoria's Supreme Court. Looking back, she speaks of the convent campaign as a career-defining experience, her favourite and most formative case. Even today, she keeps an important Abbotsford document on her desk. A campaign postcard printed with just nine words:

'It would be a sin to ruin the convent.'

The Abbotsford Convent with the city of Melbourne in the distance, 2005 (Craig Abraham/*The Age*)

Abbotsford Convent Coalition members in front of the convent. *Left to right:* Nigel Lewis, Margot Foster, Cameron McIndoe, Jo Kinross, Sally Romanes and Sue Bannerman. (Craig Abraham/*The Age*)

Members of the Abbotsford Convent Coalition. *Left to right:* Nigel Lewis, Charlotte Allen, horse (name unknown), Jo Kinross and Tony Lee. (Heath Missen/*The Age*)

Premier Steve Bracks and Minister John Thwaites under the Separation Oak, 2001. (Jason South/*The Age*)

Members of the Abbotsford Convent Coalition inspect their plans for the convent. *Left to right:* Charlotte Allen, Hilary McPhee, Nigel Lewis, Hilary Rankin, Jo Kinross and Peter Maund. (Mario Borg/*The Age*)

Before (above) and after (below): Rosina was completely covered in ivy (John Kinross)

The state of the buildings after possession, 2000 (above) (Ming Tee) and the space reclaimed: Jill Orr, *Laundry 2019*, Temporal Proximities, Magdalen Laundry, Abbotsford Convent, 1–3 March 2019, curated by Kelli Alred (Clare Rae)

The convent today is host to a diverse range of arts and cultural events (above courtesy Anne Moffat; below courtesy Charlie Kinross)

The convent lawns and courtyards are favoured gathering places (above and below courtesy Charlie Kinross)

Restoration and preservation of the historic buildings and gardens has progressed rapidly (*clockwise from top left*): courtyard of the convent building, as seen from the cloister, Rosina and the convent building (Mark Hanlin)

Timeline

c. 70,000 years ago: The First Australians spread across the continent, developing a vibrant culture and a rich tradition of agriculture and land management.

1770: Captain James Cook visits the east coast of the continent of Australia. Despite tens of thousands of years of Indigenous history and ownership, Cook claims the land for Britain.

1788: First Fleet.

31 July 1796: Mother Mary of St Euphrasia is born Rose Virginia Pelletier in Noirmoutier in the Bay of Biscay.

June 1835: John Batman's so-called treaty is 'signed' on 6 June. Of a point upstream from the Yarra's mouth, he notes in his diary on 8 June: 'This will be the place for a village.' (Batman would leave his party at Indented Head and return to Launceston.)

26 August 1835: The New South Wales governor, Sir Richard Bourke, declares Batman's treaty invalid and the settlers at Port Phillip to be trespassers.

29 August 1835: John Pascoe Fawkner's party, which had sailed from Launceston on the *Enterprize* on 12 July, sets up a settlement just below Yarra Falls. (Fawkner doesn't join the party until 16 October.)

2 September 1835: Batman's men travel to the settlement site, where they find Fawkner's party.

- 1837: Following strict regulations, Robert Hoddle lays out the distinctive grid design of the city of Melbourne.

- 1863: The Sisters of the Good Shepherd purchase Abbotsford House as the home of their new community.

- 22 July 1863: Bishop James Goold says mass at Abbotsford on the Feast of St Mary Magdalen.

- 26 August 1863: The convent officially opens.

- 11 November 1863: Ellen Fennessy (later Sister Mary of St Euphrasie) is received into the novitiate at Abbotsford, the first Australian to join the new foundation.

- Easter Sunday, 1864: The first lay sister is received at Abbotsford. The nuns give her the name of Sister Mary of St Francis Assisi.

- 1865: Towards the end of the year, two more sisters and a postulant arrive from Angers. They are Sister Mary of St Ignatius (Doyle), sister of the convent's foundress and first prioress; Mother Mary of St Joseph; Sister Mary of St Agnes (Roche); and Hannah Corbett, the sister of Sister Mary of St Francis (Xavier).

- 1867: 'Mr O'Grady, M.L.A., directed attention to the ample report published for the year 1867 of the proceedings of the Nuns. Within four years, 248 female penitents were admitted, and 170 discharged reclaimed, and fitted for the pursuit of honest and good livelihoods. In addition, from the neglected and criminal female classes, no less than 50 were discharged to earn industrious bread. The expenses of the establishment in 1867 were £4,600, and toward that amount there were received only £3,100, including £700 the product of the Penitents' labour, thus leaving a balance of £1,500 on the year. The Nuns were now in debt to the extent of £4,800. To liquidate it, they needed the aid of those present and those absent.' [*The Advocate*, 21 March 1868, p. 6]

November 1867: 'One lady, a native of Australia, has joined the order, so that the community at present numbers twelve members, exclusive of postulate.' [*Illustrated Australian News for Home Readers* (Melbourne), 26 November 1867, p. 12]

1868: 'The community at present numbers ten professed nuns and three lay sisters. During the five years of its existence there have been admitted to the Magdalen Asylum 248 reclaimed females, and 169 discharged. Of those who have taken their departure, the greater number were placed in respectable service, restored to their friends, or married; while the remainder … left voluntarily, were discharged as ineligible, went to the hospital, or died. During the same period 155 children were received into the Industrial Reformatory and Preservation Schools, and 41 discharged. At the end of the year 1867, the Magdalen Asylum contained 79 inmates, and the other institutions 84. The institution is chiefly supported by an annual grant from Parliament and voluntary contributions … With the exception of another of rather limited capabilities, recently established at Geelong, the Abbotsford Asylum is the only one of its kind in the colony of Victoria.' [*Illustrated Australian News for Home Readers* (Melbourne), 13 June 1868, p. 4]

1880: *Abandoned toddler* 'Some person or persons unknown wilfully exposed a female infant at the gates of the Abbotsford Convent, about 6.30 a.m. on the 7th instant. Description—A well-nourished female child, about 18 months old, stout build, fair hair, and blue eyes; wore a grey frock, pink cotton pinafore, white sun-bonnet, low shoes, and white socks. It was well wrapped up in a … shawl. A bundle containing two flannel night-gowns, one flannel petticoat, a calico chemise, a white petticoat, a white worked pinafore, a blue and white cotton frock, a pair of white stays, and a pair of cotton socks, to fit the child, was found near it.' [*Mercury and Weekly Courier* (Vic.), 17 April 1880, p. 2]

'Emily Bywater was charged on remand, at the Collingwood Police Court this morning, with abandoning her female child, whereby its life was endangered …

'John Carroll, a labourer working at the Abbotsford Convent, gave evidence that he found the child about two yards from the Convent gate at 6 o'clock on the morning of the 7th April, 1880. It was dressed and a shawl lay beside it. A bundle, containing clothes, was also on the ground. The morning was cold, but the grass was quite dry. Witness took the infant to the police station.

'Margaret Evans, a married woman, stated that she had nursed the child from the 3rd December, 1879, to March the following year, on which latter date she went to the home of a Mrs Fox, living at St. Kilda, at whose place the prisoner worked at the time as a domestic servant, and returned the child to her. The reason for this action was that the prisoner was in arrears in her payments for the nursing of the child. Witness saw Emily Bywater on the 12th April and was then informed by her that the child had been left outside the gate of the Abbotsford Convent. The prisoner said "I rang the bell and then went into a dark corner so that no one could see me and I saw a nun come out and take the child." … The bench said that though the prisoner deserved severe punishment for her conduct, they believed that she had not abandoned her child with the intention of injuring it, and taking into consideration her previous good character they discharged her.' [*The Herald*, 28 September 1880, p. 3]

1888: *Infant left at the Convent* 'At a quarter past 11 o'clock on Monday evening, Constable Carter, while on duty in Chalmers-street, Collingwood, heard the cry of an infant. On proceeding in the direction whence it came, he found a male child on the doorstep of the Abbotsford Convent. It was wrapped in a piece of grey blanket, and there was nothing to give a clue to whom it belonged. It was brought before the local court on Tuesday morning, and remanded for seven days.' [*The Argus*, 3 October 1888, p. 12]

1890: The Good Shepherds in the Southern Hemisphere now qualify as a separate province, with provincial headquarters at Abbotsford. The new province is to be headed by Mother Mary of the Visitation (formerly Mother Mary of St Edith [Kennedy]).

20 March 1891: On Palm Sunday, Mother Mary of St Edith is formally installed in her new position as Mother Provincial of the new Southern Province. She assumes the name Mother Mary of the Visitation.

1893: 'The Abbotsford "Home," with its large area of ground and four groups of buildings cost over £30,000. The Victorian Government aided the good work of the Sisters by a grant of £750, and when again appealed to in 1867 and 1870, the Government gave two grants of £300 each. Since then the Magdalen Asylum has kept growing with steady growth and its inmates multiplying. Since its opening, 2656 penitent souls have found shelter within the institution. Many of these have been restored to home and friends; some died happy deaths within the Asylum; while others were provided with the means to go to other lands, there to begin a new life far from old haunts and old associates. In addition to the Abbotsford Refuge, the Sisters located near Melbourne have for several years conducted an Industrial School for poor neglected children, of whom they have at present over 300 under their care. For a long time the nuns wished to be able to make a perfect separation between the Reformatory and Industrial Schools, but could not accomplish this desire till 1883, when the young Reformatory girls were transferred to the beautiful premises at Oakleigh, prepared by the Melbourne Community at a cost of £13,000, on a property of 54 acres generously given by the late Archbishop Goold. The next branch house from Abbotsford was that of "St. Magdala," Christchurch, New Zealand, founded in 1886. So well has the work of the Good Shepherd prospered in this mission that the Government has marked its appreciation by a special allowance of £500 to the institution. To make room for the increasing number of poor penitents, the Magdalen Asylum at Abbotsford, being overcrowded, a new convent has been established at Beaconsfield Parade, South Melbourne, where accommodation has been provided for nearly 100 more penitents. This new branch had cost over £15,000. The nuns have always had the support of not only the Government, but the charitable public at large, who rarely forget, even in their last bequests, the Good Shepherd charities.' [*Freeman's Journal* (Sydney), 29 April 1893, p. 15]

1894: *A letter to the Editor from the Sisters, pleading for assistance* 'The continued depression has been so keenly felt at the Convent of the Good Shepherd, Abbotsford, that we beg, through your valuable columns, to ask the charitable public not to forget in their kind benefactions the inmates of the Magdalen Asylum or the neglected little ones under our care, all of whom eagerly look forward to their share of Christmas and New Year festivities.' [*The Argus*, 22 December 1894, p. 8]

1897: *Extracts from a report covering the previous year* 'In December, 1895, there were 286 children in the institution; since then there have been 205 admissions and re-admissions; 177 service and other homes were secured during the year, 34 of which were situations for industrial school wards, and 91 were situations for preservatives. The 52 remaining discharges were girls sufficiently trained restored to friends, and others whose parents were enabled to resume their support. Very favourable reports have been received of most girls at service. In order to lay by a little provision for their future, and to teach them to be provident, all girls at service are caused to bank not less than one shilling every week. The children in the institution are employed as follows: About 148 attend school, which is twice a year visited by inspectors, and monthly examinations are also held by the sisters in charge. Out of lesson hours they are at needlework or household duties. Those over school age are distributed to work in the laundry, bakery, kitchen, farm and garden. The children make and mend their own clothing. The monotony of school life is frequently interrupted by special fete days of the convent and other treats kindly given by charitable visitors. The large buildings now given up for the most part to the children of the preservative class were originally erected at great expense solely for the Catholic wards of the industrial department, who at one time were committed direct to Abbotsford, but the introduction of the boarding out system, some years ago, caused an almost total withdrawal of those children, who were then distributed to foster homes throughout the colony … convent shelters 235 … children known as preservatives, while there are only 47 Industrial School wards, almost every one of whom has been sent here for training, having been found unfit to earn a livelihood after a foster home training or bringing up … The grown girls in the preservative class are such as have been placed here for the purpose of discipline and domestic training. For them, as well as for the Industrial School girls, situations are readily obtained, in fact the number of applicants for servants far exceeds the number of girls eligible for service …' [*The Age*, 7 January 1897, p. 6]

1903: The Abbotsford Convent has grown to 102 sisters (including sixteen novices).

1904: 'The Magdalen Asylum … Over 2000 names have been entered on the books of this class since the opening in September 1863. The vast majority of that number returned to the world … The books in Abbotsford show that since the Convent was opened 41 years ago, [more than 9000] names have been entered; at the present moment there are 786 for whom food and raiment are provided, in addition to 291 educated at the primary school, raising the responsibility of the Sisters to 1077 souls.

'In addition, there are flourishing branch houses providing for 122 at Oakleigh, 194 at South Melbourne, 176 at Christchurch, New Zealand, 113 at Hobart, Tasmania, 58 at the new Convent opened at Perth … and a magnificent orphanage building in Bendigo.' ['Work of the Good Shepherd Sisters in Australasia: Congress paper read at Abbotsford on Thursday, 27th October, 1904, by the Very Rev. Dean Phelan', *The Advocate*, 5 November 1904, p. 10]

1905: *The Protestant women's unannounced visit* 'Wishing to take the opportunity of having the most time, the visiting hours varying, we presented ourselves for admission early in the morning. On arriving I pulled the bell, and, after a few seconds, a small slide was opened, and a nun appeared, asking my name, and who I wished to see. I replied that I and my friends wished to be shown over the convent. Accordingly the door was unlocked, and we entered. The first thing we noticed was a very large image of the Virgin Mary surrounded by flowers and pot plants, also crucifixes, and arranged about were candles. There was a long hall or veranda, extending about 50 feet, enclosed on one side by glass windows. Hung on the walls were beautiful Scriptural paintings. On the floor were ferns and pot plants, and a few chairs, that gave the appearance of comfort and taste. From this hall we were escorted into a very large reception room, which had large double doors that opened into another similar room. The two could easily be converted into a large ballroom. The floors were polished, and handsome rugs lay about. Here and there were small tables bearing marble crucifixes. An image of our Saviour, a very beautiful piece of work, was standing over the mantelpiece; on the walls were Scriptural paintings and a portrait of Archbishop Carr.

'We were kept waiting about five minutes for the Mother Superior, who, on making her appearance, asked me the names of my lady friends, and appeared pleased to have the opportunity of showing us around. Sister Gabriel (secretary) accompanied us. The first place we entered was a schoolroom, which was large and airy, and accommodated girls from 10 years and upwards. Their teachers were nuns. The Mother Superior spoke to some of the girls, asking if they were well looked after. There were other questions that I should have liked to ask myself, but did not get the chance. I noticed how sad the girls looked, so very different to the children outside. The first thing they did when we entered the door of the schoolroom was to stand to order, and they did it well; in fact, I am of opinion they are made to do all things well. In another schoolroom the children ranged in age from four years to ten. Oh, you should have seen their sad faces. I shall never forget their expressions. They were not very tidy, in fact, some of their clothing was not very clean, and some had very dirty boots on. I suspect these children are orphans. I fancy they do their own mending, by the look of the torn pinafores they wore. Some of them recited very nicely; and several sang to us. I was so touched by their appearance that it made me feel rather miserable. The Mother Superior asked them did they ever get the cane? and they answered, "Yes. Mother." Then she asked, "And what do you say to your teacher after?" "I deserved it, teacher." Thus are they trained to believe that whatever is done to them it is quite right. Just fancy our saying we deserved a caning after being beaten, and being made to say it as these children have to do.

'Next, we were taken into the chapel. It is richly furnished about the altar, which was decorated with flowers and images, but it appeared to my mind as some other place than God's house of worship. The two nuns knelt down, and crossed themselves, but we just looked on. I noticed three or four nuns doing penance, or I suppose they were. They looked so white and sad that I soon retired. It was then discovered by the Mother Superior that we were Protestants.

'I asked to see the folding and packing room, a place where all clothes are sorted over. To this part of the building the entrance was two large gates, which were locked. The Mother Superior opened these with a key, which was attached to a cord or chain around her waist. I made a remark to her about these gates being locked. “Oh,” she said, “they are not often locked,” but I thought different. Anyhow, there were three or four young girls folding up clothes, and a nun with them. I presume so that they should be kept at their work. We also went upstairs above this room to the bedroom, which was very large and airy. It contained about 50 beds side by side. The counterpanes were dark and pinned down at each corner. I am sorry I did not undo these coverlids, and find out if they were clean, and soft to lie down on. However, I did not, so must give them the benefit of any doubt. We visited a place where the cakes, biscuits, or pastry are made. They had fitted up in this room a range with the latest improvements. We were shown samples of biscuits and cakes, but did not taste them. They looked nice. I noticed a steam boiler as we passed out, and seeing no one in attendance, I mentioned this, and asked if anyone in particular attended to it. The Mother Superior answered, “Oh, we all take a turn.” Then I asked if they had a certificate? “Oh yes we have,” she replied. I told her if such a thing was done outside there would be trouble, for no one is allowed to attend a boiler unless they hold a certificate. We then proceeded to the dining-room which was a very long one and arranged the whole length was a table placed in the centre, with forms on either side. Each serviette contained a spoon, knife and fork, butter and bread, wrapped up. Nearby was a large mug placed for each one. I thought this room looked very presentable, and enticing to one’s appetite. I am given to understand that if any of the workers do anything out of the way, or are slow at work, they do not receive any meat or butter at meal times.

‘The next place was the steam laundry. We had to pass through gates again. They, too, were locked. Many women were working in this room. There seemed every convenience for the work, but the women’s faces were sad, and they worked as if every minute was precious. I asked the Mother Superior about the payment they received for doing this work. She answered, “The best price outside, and we can prove it to the authorities.” All the more reason they should pay for water used and pay wages, and have the eight hours’ working system. After passing out of those gates they were at once locked. The time had now passed for, it was 11.20, and the Mother Superior was escorting us back to the reception room. I stopped and asked to be taken to the soap and boot department. This caused a surprise. The Mother had no idea I knew so much, but she did not seem very willing, and made out she had a very important appointment at 11.30, but said she would be only too pleased if I would come again. I was not to be got rid of so easily, however. At last they consented, but sarcastically remarked "did I think they were not prepared to show us these places, as if they had something they did not wish us to see?" When we came to the first place, the gate, as usual, had to be unlocked. The soap room was small. I notice on entering another steam boiler. No one was attending to this. The steam was up to 40. I looked at the glass, for I understand a little about it. There was a young girl pouring out the soap liquid from a tap. A nun was looking on. I did not see anyone in attendance for the boiler, but thought it wise not to mention this, though I consider it out of place and anything but complying with our laws as to certificated engine drivers. Above this room is the boot-making department. I saw about four girls and three large boot-machines, quite enough tools to provide for 300 people. One young woman was mending boots, and had a box full of repairs. Another was cutting out tops, so I was quite convinced that they do all that is wanted for the whole of the inmates. In both these rooms a nun was present, so these women have very little chance to speak to one another, or even to visitors. We agreed amongst ourselves before entering the convent that we would ask any of the inmates if they wished to come out. I unfortunately found no chance. The Mother Superior kept so close to me that a young girl would get no chance to speak. One of my lady friends asked one young girl in the boot department if she wished to come out, and she quickly replied, "My God, I do," and gave her name. This happened while I happened to be talking with the nuns. One must be sharp to do anything unnoticed by these nuns. If I had only known that one inmate expressed a desire to come out while I was inside the convent, I should have done all that was legal to have taken her out with me. I was only informed after I got outside about this girl, as also of another in the fancy work department. I saw some young girls wheeling barrows, also painting fences and doing many things that are rather unusual for women.

'In passing through one of the rooms I noticed scaffolding suspended overhead. At each end was a paint pot. I was just wondering who could be painting the ceiling, when the Mother Superior mentioned that two young men were doing the painting. She mentioned their absence, and thought they had gone away for a cup of tea, in fact, she turned round to me and said, "perhaps you don't believe we employ men to do some work?" I replied laughingly that I would know a man if I saw him. With that she ordered a nun to find them. After a few seconds they made their appearance, and were told that I appeared doubtful that men were working in the next room. They exclaimed readily that they had gone away for some tea. I smiled at them and said I was satisfied now as to their being men.

'We then passed on to the ironing room. It seemed a very busy room. Strange to say, as soon as we made our appearance, the girls began to sing, and nearly everyone joined in. Whatever they were singing it was most impressive to hear the different voices blending. I got the idea that this singing was started so that we should not talk to the girls. I was watching my opportunity to ask one if she was happy, because she did not sing. I took my chance when we got by the door and the nuns were outside, for I ran back again and asked this girl. The reply I got was that she was happy; but at the same time I do not believe it. On two occasions I tried some doors to see if they were unfastened. I was spoken to for doing so by the Mother Superior. The various departments are cut off from communication one with the other by gates, all of which are kept locked.

'The Mother Superior thought I ought to support and help them in every way, as they give their lives for charity, and to help poor fallen women. I told her we did that outside, but no institution in Victoria was under lock and key except the Melbourne Gaol and Pentridge. I was asked if I and my friends would give a donation. I replied on their behalf "No." We were escorted back to the reception room, where the Mother Superior asked the sister nun to get the visitors' book. Two of my friends were asked to sign and replied "Yes"; but I refused, to the astonishment of the nuns.

'I feel very dissatisfied that women should be in a supposed charitable institution under lock and key in every particular, and no limit to their hours of working under the Factories Act, or any wages paid for work done, and I intend to work quietly, with a strong determination to assist in having an alteration made in the Abbotsford Convent regulations, without bringing religion into the question.' [*The Watchman*, 28 January 1905, p. 4]

1909: The Victorian treasurer, together with members of both houses of state parliament and local councillors from Collingwood and Fitzroy, visits the convent following an appeal for governmental assistance from Mother Mary of St Alphonsus.

19 December 1910: 'A sparrow's nest underneath the slate roof of a big brick building used as a laundry became ignited through a defective boiler flue having been overheated, and portion of the ceiling and roof of the laundry was severely damaged … The chief officer (Mr H. B. Lee) and 19 firemen responded to the alarm … and the flames were got under control in 10 minutes.' [*The Argus*, 20 December 1910, p. 8]

1914: *Fiftieth anniversary of opening of convent* The anniversary was celebrated on the Feast of St Augustine, 28 August, with a 'spiritual festival', the chief feature of which 'was the devotion of the Forty Hours' Adoration of the Blessed Sacrament, with its accompanying majestic and imposing ceremonial'. This was accompanied by a 'family festival' across 'the convent's various departments, each "class" enjoying its own auspicious celebrations of the golden jubilee'. The festivities also included the convent's employees, 'for the members of this much respected and deserving body (whose long, devoted services and proverbial integrity as carpenters, gardeners, drivers, engineers, etc … have well merited praise and grateful appreciation in highest measure) were recipients of a thoughtful mark of esteem from the nuns'. The convent's employees were invited to a dinner in the convent. The 'place of honour at "the festival board"' was 'unanimously accorded to Mr Edward Nolan, who has honourably and indefatigably filled the position of head carpenter on the premises for well-nigh the whole term of fifty years. Moreover, each of this man's sons, as his school course was duly completed, came to "Abbotsford" to acquire earliest experience in the trade under this estimable father's excellent training and proving themselves ever worthy of the trust reposed in them by the Sisters of the Good Shepherd.' In 'remembrance of their long association with the convent, Mr Nolan had the additional satisfaction of seeing his family assembled with him as guests at the jubilee celebration'. [*The Advocate*, 4 April 1914, p. 16]

1926: *Infant left in garden* 'A newly-born child was found on a lawn in front of a house in Clarke street, Collingwood, near the Abbotsford Convent, warmly clad with a tin of lactogen and a feed bottle by its side. A note addressed to the Reverend Mother of the Abbotsford Convent asked her to take the child, stating: "I am leaving my child as I am out of work and cannot find a soul to take care of it. Her name is Elvie McB?, birthday is April 4th." The child was taken to the Children's Home at Carlton.' [*Barrier Miner* (Broken Hill), 19 April 1926]

1929: *Fiftieth anniversary of St Euphrasia's School* 'Past pupils were invited to celebrate the 50th anniversary of the opening of St Euphrasia's School at a breakfast and Holy Communion to "be held on Sunday, April 28, at 8.30 am". Those unable to attend were urged to "participate in spirit by receiving Holy Communion, and thus form the golden links of an unbroken chain of union and prayer".' [*The Advocate*, 11 April 1929, p. 30]

1929: *Abbotsford Convent Golden Jubilee Ball* 'Festoons of vari-coloured streamers and scarves, caught up at intervals with dainty baskets of flowers and shaded electric bulbs, lent a carnival air to the Collingwood Town Hall on Tuesday, June 11, when the members of St. Euphrasia's Past Pupils' Association held a grand Golden Jubilee ball.

'The president of the old girls, Mrs M. Bolger was gowned in French pleated black georgette, worn under a black ring velvet bridge coat; … the vice-presidents were Miss Vera King, wearing apple green georgette; Miss Lena Flynn, bois de rose satin and georgette; Miss Annie Nelson, white French beaded georgette; Mrs J. Merner, black silk, spotted net, with bustle bow in pastel shaded taffeta ribbon …' [*The Advocate*, 20 June 1929, p. 33]

1934: *Flooding* 'A subscription list has been opened at Collingwood Town Hall in aid of the Abbotsford Convent and Industrial School, which suffered damage estimated at £2000 in the recent floods, losing much fencing and property as well as having the vegetable gardens attached to the institution ruined. There are 700 inmates at the institution, women and children, and the loss of the gardens in themselves will involve the convent in an additional expenditure of £50 a month for several months until fresh crops are grown.' [*The Herald*, 19 December 1934, p. 12]

1939: *St Euphrasia's sixtieth anniversary* 'On April 14, 1879, St. Euphrasia's School was opened at the Convent of the Good Shepherd, Abbotsford, and to celebrate the 60th anniversary of their alma mater the Past Pupils' Association will hold a diamond jubilee ball at the Collingwood Town Hall on Wednesday, June 14 ... A debutante set will be presented, and those who wish to join should communicate with the president (Miss Noreen Clancey, F 2792). Tickets are now available, and may be obtained from the hon. secretary (Mrs. Irena Trapp, 62 Sydney-street, Collingwood), who will also be pleased to give full information about the ball. To augment the ball funds a dance will be held at the Green Door Cabaret, Collins-street, on Saturday, March 25. Subscription, 2/6.' [*The Advocate*, 23 March 1939, p. 33]

May 1940: St Mary Euphrasia Pelletier is canonised in Rome.

1947: *Death of Mother Mary of the Visitation (Kennedy)* 'Founder of most of the Convents of the Good Shepherd in Australia, Mother Mary of the Visitation died at the Abbotsford Convent of the Order today in her 96th year.

'Born in Ireland, she came to Australia 73 years ago, two years after she had taken her vows in France, where the supreme body of the Order is located. About 40 years ago she became Mother Superior—head of the Order in Australia. For the last six years she has lived in retirement at the Abbotsford Convent. Solemn Requiem Mass will be celebrated at the Chapel of the Abbotsford Convent at 10.30 a.m. on Monday and the funeral will then leave for the Boroondara Cemetery, Kew.' [*The Herald*, 19 September 1947, p. 5]

Obituary of Mother Mary 'On Friday, September 19, at the Abbotsford Convent, Mother Mary of the Visitation Kennedy passed peacefully to her eternal reward … The late regretted Mother was born on June 18, 1852, at Ballyneale, Co. Tipperary, Ireland, her parents being Michael Kennedy and Mary Nugent. She entered the Good Shepherd Convent at Waterford and went thence to the Mother House of the Congregation at Angers, France, for her novitiate. To the then very far distant Australia she came in 1874, arriving on Christmas Day. Strength, personality and energy combined to render this young nun zealous for the fulfilment of her recently-made vow to work for the salvation of souls, a welcome addition to the little community that had arrived in Melbourne 11 years previously. So much so, that when a foundation was made in Christchurch, New Zealand, in 1886, she was chosen its first Superior. How well she laid those foundations is now seen in the many works for souls undertaken in that convent.

'In 1890, the Australian Houses of the Order were constituted a separate province, and Mother Mary of the Visitation returned to Abbotsford as first Provincial Superior. This office she held, with a short intermission, until 1921. During that time she made foundations in South Melbourne, Hobart, Perth, Bendigo and Sydney. Until 1936, she was Superior of Rosary Place, South Melbourne.

'The last ten years of her life were spent at Abbotsford, where she brought to the role of Mary the same wholehearted vitality that had distinguished her active years. Successively, the Sisters and her friends celebrated the golden, diamond and ruby jubilees of her religious profession. The last, in 1943, was enhanced by the celebration of Solemn High Mass by the Carmelite Fathers … those who experienced the warmth of her hospitality and the strength of her sympathy … Mass was celebrated at the convent on Monday, September 22, by his Grace Most Rev. Dr Mannix. Present in the sanctuary were their Lordships Right Rev. Dr McCarthy, Right Rev. Dr Vesters, Right Rev. Dr O'Collins, Right Rev. Dr Stewart, and Right Rev. Mgr. Fox, as well as some 60 of the reverend clergy and Sisters of Religious Orders. Such a manifestation of esteem for their late Mother was a consolation to the Sisters.' [*The Advocate*, 1 October 1947, p. 15]

1949: *Fire in the laundry* 'Fire yesterday morning destroyed the top floor and roof of the Abbotsford Convent laundry, causing £5,000 damage … None of the laundry was destroyed by the fire, and the bottom floor and machinery are intact.

'About 20 girls and two supervising sisters were in the laundry when smoke was noticed coming from the drying department. Ten minutes afterwards the fire had a firm grip. Fire brigades from Fitzroy and Collingwood attended the outbreak, and had it under control in half an hour. Cause of the fire is not known.' [*The Argus*, 17 September 1949, p. 5]

1952: *Boys chasing convent cows* 'A good big watchdog would be welcomed by the Sisters at the Good Shepherd Convent, Abbotsford, to keep away boys who chase cows in the convent garden. Most warm days boys swim across the Yarra and cut through convent fences, Sister Mary, who is in charge of the convent, said today. Then they chase cows across the paddock and try to herd them into the convent garden. At night boys steal into the garden and help themselves to lettuce, tomatoes, carrots and parsnips. Not satisfied, they pull up dozens of plants and leave them to die.

'"A few weeks ago one of our best cows died through injuries received when the boys chased it," said Sister Mary. "We have chased the boys but they always get away by swimming the river. Police never arrive in time to catch them."' [*The Herald*, 7 April 1952, p. 9]

1954: *Hoses slashed* 'During the week-end somebody slashed three hoses at the Convent of the Good Shepherd, Clarke Street, Abbotsford. The motive might have been vandalism, theft (a length of hose was stolen), or rage because the convent's sprinklers were playing during the ban. The rage would not have been justified. The convent gets its garden water straight from the Yarra.' [*The Herald*, 18 January 1954, p. 2]

24 April 1955: In 'accordance with the wishes of Our Very Hon. Mother General', a section known as the Juniorate is established for newly professed sisters. A room set aside for this at Abbotsford is made 'bright and comfortable'. [Catherine Kovesi, *Pitch Your Tents on Distant Shores* (Caringbah: Playright Publishing, 2010), p. 274]

1956: 'Every year for the last 30 the chaps from Tattersall's Club have played Santa Claus for the girls out at the Abbotsford Convent—and this Christmas was no exception. They were out there in force with £300 worth of presents for the youngsters and as usual they had a wonderful time. There are 160 girls at that convent—from toddlers up. Some of them are quite small, but they've still seen something I've never seen. A bookmaker playing Father Christmas.' [*The Argus*, 26 December 1956, p. 1]

1963: The convent celebrates its centenary.

8 May 1965: Our Lady of Lourdes Commercial School opens.

1967: Despite the changes taking place within their order, the sisters continue to minister to women in need. 'One of the most tragic in this period was a former member of the Sacred Heart Class, Mrs Cecilia Ryan, who travelled from her home in New South Wales in January 1967 to be near her son, Ronald Ryan, who had been condemned to hang at Pentridge Gaol on the first Friday of February. The Ryan family had come under the care of sisters at Abbotsford over many years. Not only Ronald's mother, but also two of his sisters had spent time in the various Classes at Abbotsford. Cecilia Ryan stayed at Abbotsford "to seek solace and understanding sympathy", and to try and escape some of the relentless attention of the media. The prison chaplain who ministered to Ryan in the weeks and the minutes leading up to his death was Father John Brosnan, referred to in prison jargon as a "sky pilot". As Official Chaplain to the Victorian State Prisons, Brosnan lived at the priests' cottage at Abbotsford and regularly said Mass for the community. Under Father Brosnan's guidance, the Sisters of the Good Shepherd continued what has become one of their enduring activities—visitation to prisons. Also visiting Ronald Ryan was Sister Margaret Kingston … Ryan wrote many letters to Sr Margaret. Although he had been baptised a Catholic, Ronald was no longer a practising Catholic. Before his death, however, he returned to his faith … When he was questioned as to how his faith had been rekindled, he replied that it was due to "a Saintly Nun [Sister Margaret] and a knockabout priest [Father Brosnan]". Sister Margaret became known affectionately by the inmates at Pentridge as "Sister Alias". This was due to the fact that her ministry there coincided with the decision amongst the sisters first to drop the prefatory "Mary" from their names, and then, in most cases, to adopt their baptismal names.' [Kovesi, pp. 297–8]

1967: *Ronald Ryan* 'Earlier today Ryan told his family, his mother, Mrs Cecilia Ryan, 75, his sisters, Gloria and Irma, and his priest, Father John Brosnan, he was resigned to die.

'"It took a knockabout priest and a saintly nun to do it", Ryan told his mother. "But I'm ready to go."

'Father Brosnan, the Roman Catholic chaplain at Pentridge Gaol is the "knockabout priest" and Sister Madonna [sic], of the Convent of the Good Shepherd, in Abbotsford, the "saintly nun". Father Brosnan received Ryan, a Catholic who had given up his faith, back into his church and Sister Madonna [sic] attended Mrs Ryan.' [*Canberra Times*, 31 January 1967, p. 4]

'Ronald Ryan told a Melbourne nun shortly before he was executed that he shot to wound but not kill a warder, Mr George Hodson, during a Pentridge Prison escape 20 years ago. Sister Margaret Kingston, of the Good Shepherd convent in suburban Abbotsford, said yesterday that Mr Ryan had also told her his conscience was clear. In 1967, Mr Ryan became the last person to be hanged in Australia after he was convicted of shooting Mr Hodson during the 1965 jail break. Sister Kingston said, "He told me, I shot to wing, I didn't shoot to kill." She said she accompanied Mr Ryan's mother when she visited her son at Pentridge during the five weeks before the execution. "The law had condemned him, but his conscience had freed him," Sister Kingston said.' [*Canberra Times*, 13 June 1986, p. 7]

1971: A consultant calculates that a total of 346 girls between the ages of eleven and eighteen reside in all the institutions in the order's Australasian province, and an additional fifty-nine children are at St Aidan's Orphanage. The total number of women cared for is 439, aged twenty-one to ninety. Of these 439, 61 per cent are in the order's four Victorian houses, with Abbotsford accounting for 32 per cent of the total. Of the 270 sisters in the province, 48 per cent are aged over sixty, and 64 per cent over fifty. In the decade 1962 to 1972, only thirty-five new novices enter and remain within the order.

1973: From February, St Euphrasia's Primary School is staffed with lay teachers under a lay principal.

1975: The remains of the convent's foundress and first prioress, Mother Mary of St Joseph (Doyle), along with those of the other pioneering nuns buried onsite, are transferred to Boroondara Cemetery and laid to rest in the Abbotsford Community plot. Mother Mary of Mt Carmel (Curtain) remains entombed in the crypt under the chapel (her memorial stone is set in the floor of the main aisle).

3 December 1977: The Archbishop of Melbourne, Sir Frank Little, lays the foundation stone for the new smaller convent building and nursing home.

1980: In March, pursuant to the *Urban Land Authority Act 1979*, the Victorian Urban Land Authority (ULA) replaces the old Urban Land Council. The Act empowers the ULA to provide development allotments as directed by the planning minister, facilitate the disposal of surplus land held by the Crown and statutory bodies, and assist in the implementation of state urban planning policies and major state projects. The ULA's powers include buying, selling, subdividing and consolidating land; granting leases and licences; and constructing roads and other infrastructure, such as drains and sewers.

1986: 'Victorian Arts Minister Race Mathews announced yesterday that the funds would allow Circus Oz to establish itself at an old convent in inner suburban Abbotsford. Mr Mathews said the premises, owned by the Lincoln Institute, would be supplied rent free … Circus Oz has been operating on a seasonal basis in various parts of Australia for eight years.' [*Canberra Times*, 20 December 1986, p. 10]

1996: La Trobe University moves its Health Sciences faculty to Bundoora.

- December 1997: The newly formed St Heliers Convent Action Group has its first meeting.

- February 1998: The St Heliers Convent Action Group becomes the Abbotsford Convent Coalition (ACC).

- March 1998: The City of Yarra abandons Planning Amendment L54 and agrees to establish a working party to consider the future of the convent.

- 1998: The ULA adopts a more commercial-sounding name, the Urban Land Corporation, while continuing to perform an unusual dual role as a property developer and an implementer of state government planning policy. The organisation subsequently becomes the Urban and Regional Land Corporation before merging with the Docklands Authority to become VicUrban and, ultimately, Places Victoria.

- 1999–2006*:* The Village Park Consortium (VPC), a joint venture between Citta Property Group and Australand Holdings Ltd, is the successful tenderer for the delivery of the Melbourne 2006 Commonwealth Games Athletes Village (later Parkville Gardens).

- 2001: Petruccelli Painting, on Nicholson Street in Abbotsford, gives the ACC an office along with the use of a telephone and a power point, at no cost to the campaign. Tony Lee furnishes the office with furniture he has rescued from a bank closure.

- October 2002: State government ministers receive more than 2000 letters of opposition to Australand's northern site proposal. Planning Minister Mary Delahunty announces a 'final compromise': 130 units up to only five storeys high along Johnston Street, no parking for the convent and 64 spaces for the Children's Farm.

- 27 April 2004: The state government formally transfers the title of the Abbotsford Convent to the Abbotsford Convent Foundation. The precinct is now in community hands.

- 2006: Maggie Maguire is appointed as the convent's first CEO.

- 2008: The federal government delivers the National Apology to the Stolen Generations on 13 February at a special ceremony at Parliament House in Canberra.

- 2008: The c3 Contemporary Art Space opens at the convent site. The upstairs section of Rosina is restored for performing arts use, supported by the federal government, Dara Foundation, Ian Potter Foundation, Helen Macpherson Smith Trust, Dyson Bequest, Robert Salzer Foundation and a number of individuals.

- 2009: The federal government delivers the National Apology to the Forgotten Australians and Former Child Migrants at a special remembrance event in Canberra on 16 November. Soon afterwards, the Sisters of the Good Shepherd apologise to those who have painful memories of their time at Good Shepherd convents.

- 2009: Restoration of the Mercator building begins with the support of the Sidney Myer Fund Commemorative Grants Program.

- 2010: The convent is accepted as a member of the prestigious European network of historical monuments that are now arts and cultural sites, Réseau Européen des Centres Culturels de Rencontre.

- 2011: Works are completed to save the Separation oak.

- 2012: Kerry Greenwood's *Unnatural Habits* and Maureen McCarthy's *The Convent*—both containing fictionalised accounts of life at the convent—are published.

- 2013: The new 'Breezeway' wins the Small Project Architecture award at the Victorian Architecture Awards.

- 2015: The federal government announces that the ACF will receive a challenge grant of $2.681 million from the National Stronger Regions Fund (NSRF) to restore the Sacred Heart building. The restoration will also be funded by a $2 million donation from the Dara Foundation, as well as other funds the ACF has generated over the past decade.

- August 2016: The Victorian government announces that the ACF will receive a contribution of $2.7 million towards transforming the Magdalen Laundry.

- September 2016: Collette Brennan becomes CEO of the ACF.

- 31 August 2017: The Abbotsford Convent is added to the Australian National Heritage List.

- March 2018: The Sacred Heart building is reopened.

- June 2019: Stage 1 of the restoration works on the Magdalen Laundry are completed. The north side of the laundry becomes available for contemporary artistic activation and community use.

- June 2019: The Sacred Heart Building refurbishment wins the John George Knight Award for Heritage at the Victorian Architecture Awards.

Notes

Chapter 2—It began with lava

'rural retreats for gentlemen': Richmond and Burnley Historical Society, 'Development of Richmond from 1835', http://home.vicnet.net.au/~rbhs/files/development-of-richmond-from-1835.pdf, accessed October 2019.

'His daughter Elizabeth, who was eight … travel to town for his business and political activities': Samuel Furphy, *Edward M Curr and the Tide of History* (Canberra: ANU E Press, 2013), p. 47.

'mountain farm'; 'on a bare haugh and bleak bank by the side of the Tweed'; 'after the ford across the Tweed … by the monks of Melrose Abbey'; 'whimsical and picturesque': 'The House', https://www.scottsabbotsford.com/visit/the-house, accessed October 2019.

Chapter 3—Sue's kitchen

'the golden fifties': *The Herald*, 15 October 1934, p. 76.

'terrier-like': 'Battle for the Convent', The Age, 9 July 2005.

'some others of the upper class … and the "gentry" left': *Williamstown Chronicle*, 16 August 1924, p. 1.

'a section of land, about 400 acres in extent … without being exposed to south-west gales': George William Vivian, *New Lunatic Asylum: Report on the Proposed New Lunatic Asylum* (Melbourne: Printed by John Ferres, 1857), p. 3.

'a wedding-cake beauty': Carolyn Webb, 'Open House Melbourne: Former Kew asylum opens doors for rare public viewing', *The Age*, 28 June 2016.

'despite the minimal funding because supposedly we were the only people who could and would undertake a project like this': Australian Science Archives Project, 'Kew Asylum Museum / Archives', http://www.asap.unimelb.edu.au/pubs/articles/asa97/KEWA.htm, accessed October 2019.

'almost every trace of the building's past [was] eradicated': Australian Science Archives Project, 'Kew Asylum Museum/Archives,' http://www.asap.unimelb.edu.au/pubs/articles/asa97/KEWA.htm, accessed October 2019.

'fully gated residential complex'; 'tranquil, serene and friendly living at its best': 'Willsmere—it's a great place to live!', https://www.willsmere.net, accessed October 2019.

'creased': *The Argus*, 5 January 1946, p. 11.

'They were seen by Constables Chisholm and Hogan … forty shillings each': *The Argus*, 20 February 1884, p. 7.

'The gathering of fruit was in full swing … it was found that one of them was missing': *The Argus*, 17 January 1905, p. 7.

'fish with feathers': author interview with Charlotte Allen, 4 December 2018.

Chapter 4—Neither pot nor pan

'poorly lit public urinals, rubbish tips and breeding grounds for criminals': State Library of Victoria, 'Melbourne city grid', http://ergo.slv.vic.gov.au/explore-history/colonial-melbourne/everyday-life/melbourne-city-grid, accessed October 2019.

'Even if a woman took only one paying customer … she would earn more in a week than as a skilled tailoress': Catherine Kovesi, *Pitch Your Tents on Distant Shores* (Caringbah: Playright Publishing, 2010), p. 49.

'a House of Mercy for the protection … who find themselves unemployed': Mother Ursula Frayne, in a report to the Bishop of Melbourne, Dr James Goold, in 1858; Kovesi, p. 49, note 6.

'virtuous women [of] good character'; 'questionable morals': Kovesi, p. 49.

'While they strive after excellence themselves … sinking beneath the quicksands of what is called life': 'Work of the Good Shepherd Sisters in Australasia: Congress paper read at Abbotsford on Thursday, 27th October, 1904, by the Very Rev. Dean Phelan', *The Advocate*, 5 November 1904, p. 10.

'that there is no slavery but sin … a flame of divine love into the smoking flax': 'Work of the Good Shepherd Sisters in Australasia', *The Advocate*, 5 November 1904, p. 10.

'bring back to a life of virtue and peace … and time for repentance is at an end': *Geelong Advertiser*, 9 September 1863.

'French nuns'; '"guimpe" and "bandeaux" of unstarched linen … silver heart suspended from the neck': *The Advocate*, 6 September 1913, p. 17.

'Never found a house for our Magdalens if you … where they cannot be quite separate from the other categories': Kovesi, p. 39.

'Here it is!': Kovesi, p. 62, note 59.

'large and handsome with fine lofty rooms … profusely that the air was scented with them': Kovesi, p. 62, note 60.

'There was a magic in the answering … atmosphere which made labour a thing of joy': *The Advocate*, 6 September 1913, p. 17.

'being milked into a small jug, for want … object-lesson greatly appreciated by "the maiden all forlorn"': *The Advocate*, 6 September 1913, p. 17.

'There was a little farm here for them … after my cow arrived the other six cows were dead': *Punch*, 15 November 1900, p. 21.

'On the eve of the Good Shepherd's feast … the "lost sheep" should decidedly be kept "within the fold"'; 'The animal was conducted to the farmyard': *The Advocate*, 7 March 1914, p. 16.

'when Father England sent the first bag of coal … "Sure, didn't I know 'Abbotsford' when it hadn't even a pan, woman dear?"': *The Advocate*, 6 September 1913, p. 17.

'Now you can imagine, dear sisters, a vast house empty for three years … trembled to hear their thumping, we thought we were surrounded by ghosts': Kovesi, p. 65, note 65.

'There was no light save that lent by candles—a dim … Drink was then the curse of the city, and, worst of all, a "fashionable curse"': *The Advocate*, 6 September 1913, p. 17.

'Native cats … roamed at liberty under floors … a general scamper through the place in the fast-falling darkness': *The Advocate*, 6 September 1913, p. 17.

'The premises known as Abbotsford house, the grounds … bazaar is to be held to assist in discharging the same early in November next': *Geelong Advertiser*, 9 September 1863.

'With very few exceptions the unfortunate, penitent women … round to the homely occupation in which they are to be employed': Kovesi, p. 67, note 72.

'Sister Mary of St Euphrasie Fennessy became … the expansion of the order in the southern hemisphere': Kovesi, p. 66.

Chapter 5—A positive alternative

'Mr Allen suggested that a cut should be made from … The suggestion was referred to a committee': *The Herald*, 21 February 1933, p. 8.

Chapter 6—Growth

'imploring his aid that the suitable land … property for the "children" of her anxious solicitude': *The Advocate*, 20 September 1913, p. 16.

'so that they could separate completely the penitents from the reformatory children': Catherine Kovesi, *Pitch Your Tents on Distant Shores* (Caringbah: Playright Publishing, 2010), p. 74.

'The first stone of a new building in connection with the Magdalen Asylum … applicants who daily have to be refused admission for want of sufficient room': *Illustrated Australian News for Home Readers*, 26 November 1867, p. 12.

'penitent females'; 'fatherless and neglected and criminal children'; 'the juvenile portion of the inmates'; 'is a fine brick building, which at a distance looks like … the river is crossed by a substantial wooden bridge of recent date': *Illustrated Australian News for Home Readers*, 13 June 1868, p. 4.

'[The chancel] is lighted by two light traceried windows at either side … a large wheel window of elegant design most chastely carved': *The Advocate*, 29 April 1871, p. 6.

'not much under £4000': *The Advocate*, 29 April 1871, p. 6.

'The portion of the existing place of worship allotted to visitors … in a spire surmounted by a carved finial, at a total elevation of about fifty feet': *The Age*, 5 July 1875, p. 3.

'The large bell, which in a few days will be suspended in the tower … to her and to Him who through her vouchsafed to become our Saviour': *The Advocate*, 31 July 1880, p. 7.

'When the late Superioress of the Abbotsford Convent (Sister Mary J. Curtain) died … well-known clock and watch maker of Bourke street, and it is now in working order': *The Herald*, 20 March 1890, p. 4.

Chapter 8—A noble cause

'The late Mr O'Keefe of Abbotsford, upon his death, bequeathed … and curiously enough the principal manufacturer is one of the penitent Magdalens': *South Bourke and Mornington Journal*, 6 June 1877.

'There is now being erected at the eastern end of the convent grounds … Thursday. The buildings will not be finished for twelve or thirteen months at least': *South Bourke and Mornington Journal*, 6 June 1877.

'all the advantages of a high-class religious and secular training': 'as completely cut away from the inmates of the convent as if the school were at the west side of Melbourne'; 'Work of the Good Shepherd Sisters in Australasia: Congress paper read at Abbotsford on Thursday, 27th October, 1904 by the Very Rev. Dean Phelan', *The Advocate*, 5 November 1904, p. 10.

'This is the only Catholic reformatory in the colony, and the plan … but at present there are only thirty girls to be transferred from Abbotsford': *The Argus*, 4 March 1882, p. 11.

'the Government Reformatory for Roman Catholic girls': Catherine Kovesi, *Pitch Your Tents on Distant Shores* (Caringbah: Playright Publishing, 2010), p. 90.

'The Governor General, who was received with great cheering … under the supervision of the hon. secretary, Mr O'Connor, M.L.A., were all that could be desired': *The Argus*, 12 October 1901, p. 14.

'Never before has the Exhibition building looked so fine as at present … of sea below, and of a moving crowd endeavouring to see and hear from the balconies': *The Argus*, 12 October 1901, p. 14.

'£3315 was there and then subscribed as a substantial … Nuns of the Good Shepherd and their noble cause': Kovesi, p. 199.

'the number of applications received from penitents … since the convent was founded': *The Advocate*, 3 April 1909, p. 20.

'Last Sunday afternoon, the Very Rev. Dean Phelan, V.G., blessed … has been carried out under the direction of Mr. Robert Harper, of Abbotsford': *The Advocate*, 3 April 1909, p. 20.

'Home Lodge' purchase: *The Herald*, 18 January 1909, p. 6.

Chapter 9—Basket weavers

'just a bunch of basket weavers': 'Saving sacred ground', *The Age*, 26 July 2005.

'chardonnay drinkers': author interview with ACC members, 2018.

Chapter 10—Flooded

'Rising fifty feet in two days, it swept in one tide over the south of the city … sank, the flood being so great that the course of the river could not be followed': *The Herald*, 15 October 1934, p. 76.

'Penny by penny … Abbotsford laid out properly by an expert … This was skilfully accomplished': *The Advocate*, 20 September 1913, p. 16.

'day by day the flowers opened out in soft and tender glory': *The Advocate*, 20 September 1913, p. 16.

'gathered on the hills above, and kept watch … ready at any moment to go to their assistance': *The Advocate*, 20 September 1913, p. 16.

'the water began to find its way into the dining room of Mr W. H. Smith … all under water, and a considerable amount of damage has been done': *The Argus*, 18 October 1869, p. 5.

'During the early forenoon of Saturday a moderate rainfall descended … Good Shepherd, at Abbotsford, have already suffered very much': *Mount Alexander Mail*, 19 October 1869, p. 3.

'again suffered considerably': *Wagga Wagga Advertiser*, 26 June 1878, p. 4.

'The appearance of the river at and around Studley Park on Sunday … enclosure of the Abbotsford Convent was knocked down and completely carried away': *Weekly Times*, 23 March 1878, p. 11.

'suffered to a very great extent'; 'Situated in a sharp bend of the river, with the water coming well … a very dilapidated aspect. The trees are almost entirely covered in debris': *The Argus*, 29 July 1891, p. 8.

'turbulent, muddy Yarra'; 'a roaring, rushing torrent': *The Age*, 15 October 1923, p. 10.

'those whom the … institution shelters. Gifts and consignments … The Good Shepherd Convent, Abbotsford, Victoria Park railway station': *The Advocate*, 16 May 1935, p. 18.

Chapter 12—Life at the convent

'open for the reception of females without distinction … with the religious principles of such as are not Catholics': Catherine Kovesi, *Pitch Your Tents on Distant Shores* (Caringbah: Playright Publishing, 2010), pp. 75, 78.

'delicate fingers': *Ballarat Star*, 14 April 1923, p. 11.

'an offering of their hair'; 'Most of the penitents wore a narrow dark blue ribbon on their chest … persevered for many years. Some joined the ranks of Consecrated Children': Kovesi, p. 162.

'Madame Carandini sang … a chorus of the Haymarket Company'; 'resounding success': Kovesi, p. 70.

'she did not even scream as the machinery was loosened from her hand … conversion of our loved Penitents to whom she is so devoted': Kovesi, p. 157.

'we [the sisters] were working at midnight and I really … we never got those mountains of work down—it was terrible': Kovesi, p. 280.

'Well, in hindsight now, I think I could have done a lot more … we weren't allowed to even touch them. That made you sort of distant': Felicitas Hanrahan, RGS, interviewed by Anne Dalton, RGS, Abbotsford, 20 January 1997; quoted in Kovesi, p. 281.

'begging in the streets, in the company of criminals or in brothels or … without a home or income': *Neglected and Criminal Children's Act 1864*; see Kovesi, p. 70.

'with respectable families': Kovesi, p. 71, note 89.

'in danger of becoming wicked'; 'inmates'; 'imprisonment': Kovesi, p. 71, note 90.

'6 to 6.30: Rise, dress and make beds … 8: Night prayers, and retire in silence to bed': *The Argus*, 5 February 1869, p. 6.

'industrial children'; 'in different parts of the classroom': Kovesi, p. 71, note 91.

'kept in separate dormitories at night, one large ward … so that the children may be said to be under supervision by night as well as by day': Kovesi, p. 72, note 92.

'The eastern transept … is intended for the penitents … will be for the children of the Industrial Schools': *The Advocate*, 29 April 1871, p. 6.

'When, my dear daughters, you go by Holy Obedience … and not any other house even if, to you, it seems perfect': Sister Mary Euphrasia Pelletier, *'My Dear Daughters': Conferences and Instructions of Saint Mary Euphrasia Pelletier* (Hong Kong: Advanced Printing Co., 1994), Chapter 3, Conference 1, 28.

'each female criminal or neglected girl committed to the institution by the courts of justice': *The Advocate*, 21 May 1870, p. 8.

'The industry and the resources of the Nuns, and the generosity of the public … would cost the State double the amount given to the Nuns': *The Advocate*, 21 May 1870, p. 8.

'the mode and merits': *The Advocate*, 24 August 1872, p. 10.

'In the Government establishments the gross cost per head for … other buildings and places necessary for their good and effective work': *The Advocate*, 24 August 1872, p. 10.

'how much can be done by women under the supervision of … clean the machinery and do all other necessary work without men's assistance': *The Charities Commission: The Abbotsford Asylum* (1891), in Kovesi, p. 145.

'quiet, inoffensive'; 'She was then in excellent bodily … not any mark of violence about her': *Weekly Times*, 21 February 1885, p. 5.

'Upon reaching the convent, the mother "found the girl lying in a filthy …" in fact, to use the mother's words, "she was black and blue"': *Weekly Times*, 21 February 1885, p. 5.

'recovered somewhat, and told her mother that she … where she was found by her mother as described': *Weekly Times*, 21 February 1885, p. 5.

'there was nothing to show that the deceased was ill-treated at the convent': *Weekly Times*, 21 February 1885, p. 5.

'That the union respectfully ascertain from the Collingwood City Council … females especially, are debarred from procuring the means of an honest livelihood': *The Argus*, 10 June 1903, p. 6.

'He stated that that institution used millions of gallons of water, and never … Roman Catholic institution also received children into the orphanage and taught them to work': *The Watchman*, 29 August 1903, p. 6.

'Competition was unknown in Melbourne in the laundry trade until 1891 … was publicly blamed, while other laundries were able to do as they pleased': *The Advocate*, 5 September 1903, p. 25.

'We never interfere with the public trade ... they leave the institution, either in public laundries or in private families': *The Advocate*, 5 September 1903, p. 25.

'By no means. We know that report has gone abroad through ... burden on public charity. Such a class love work and take great interest in it': *The Advocate*, 5 September 1903, p. 25.

'Because the inmates are not able to compete. Owing ... gentle persons would never have the courage to come as they now do': *The Advocate*, 5 September 1903, p. 25.

'It is a well-known fact that we make house shoes for inmates and ... carpentering and gardening, besides the amount spent on tradesmen, repairs, etc.': *The Advocate*, 5 September 1903, p. 25.

'Yes. We have a primary school, with an average attendance of 270 on ... finding homes, and our wards are to be found in all the States doing and earning well': *The Advocate*, 5 September 1903, p. 25.

'Not the least objection. It is well known that the institution ... of improvement, and for the additional comfort of the inmates': *The Advocate*, 5 September 1903, p. 25.

'Canon Berry at the outset referred to certain statements made by ... in an article by him which appeared in the "National Review" for last month': *The Age*, 11 September 1903, p. 6.

'handsome'; 'looked nice'; 'young girls wheeling barrows': *The Watchman*, 28 January 1905, p. 4.

'I, Ella Laughton, was born at Penhurst, September 2nd, 1875, and ... constantly on the watch to prevent any getting away, or attempting to escape': *The Watchman*, 24 June 1905, p. 1.

'T.A.R.—, J.P., who so modestly refrained from disclosing his identity in this unsavoury case': *The Advocate*, 1 July 1905, p. 16.

'T. A. Rogers, the accredited representative of the "Watchman" ... frequently mentioned in the paper in connection with several Orange functions': *The Advocate*, 1 July 1905, p. 16.

'primary loyalty to the Pope': Kovesi, p. 150.

'Sir, I respectfully beg to inform you that I was an inmate of ... Yours, etc., (Mrs) Isabella Jessop. Stafford-street, 22nd January': *The Age*, 25 January 1907, p. 6.

'surprise visit': *The Age*, 1 February 1907, p. 5.

'on account of building': *The Age*, 1 February 1907, p. 5.

'The cost per bed during last year was ... institution is managed economically'; 'special charges': *The Age*, 1 February 1907, p. 5.

'surprise visit'; 'did not do that sort of thing': *The Age*, 1 February 1907, p. 5.

'It is a fact, however, that, like all that officer's, … not be specially prepared for by the institutions he is to visit': *The Age*, 1 February 1907, p. 5.

'Speaking at the Collingwood Mission meeting on Sunday … ourselves to any party intent on stirring up sectarian strife in our midst': *The Advocate*, 9 February 1907, p. 16.

'a fanatical crank': *The Advocate*, 2 March 1907; *Freeman's Journal*, 14 March 1907, p. 18.

'Dr Mannix said that women and girls housed there were put … undercut in prices, and because it did not it had lost many orders': *The Age*, 21 August 1922, p. 11.

'alongside mental derelicts': *The Herald*, 31 October 1952, p. 5.

'The explanation in each instance was that the girls' work could … Those with talent are encouraged to go on to secondary education': *The Herald*, 31 October 1952, p. 5.

Chapter 14—Coming and going

'hasty knocking'; 'two females, in what appeared as nuns' habits, rushed into … was the plain, impromptu explanation courteously given by the Lady Superior': *Kilmore Free Press*, 9 May 1878, p. 3; *Portland Guardian*, 9 May 1878, p. 3; et al.

'A young girl named Ellen Molony was apprehended yesterday … court the next morning, "Sergeant Bell applied for her discharge, which was granted"': *The Herald*, 12 November 1888, p. 8.

'in the costume worn by the inmates of the Convent of the Good Shepherd'; 'in a drunken fit'; 'Being in destitute circumstances'; 'motherly instincts'; 'She resolved to escape': *Ballarat Star*, 26 April 1890, p. 4.

'dressed in a striped costume': *The Herald*, 15 October 1915, p. 10.

'rather attractive-looking young girl of 18'; 'riding astride the ridge': *The Sun*, 8 April 1923, p. 2.

'bristling with broken glass set in cement'; 'They avoided injury as much as possible by placing pieces … and dropped to the other side. They were badly shaken and bruised': *The Sun*, 12 April 1923, p. 9.

'leading a respectable life'; 'bluffed': *The Age*, 16 April 1927, p. 19.

'Too right I can': *The Advocate*, 16 April 1927, p. 5.

'absconded'; 'hurried along various streets in Abbotsford … They were returned to the convent': *The Age*, 16 February 1929, p. 26.

'The girl disappeared from the casualty ward at … where she had been taken for treatment': *The Herald*, 7 January 1930, p. 2.

Chapter 16—The end of an era

'The only parts of the establishment to be shared by the two … "St Peter's Community", and the other for the new "St Paul's Community"': Catherine Kovesi, *Pitch Your Tents on Distant Shores* (Caringbah: Playright Publishing, 2010), p. 304.

'to make suggestions for the development of [the] Apostolate to suit modern conditions': Kovesi, p. 304.

'It is now well over one hundred years since the Magdalen Laundry … whom they were helping to become useful and happy citizens when they return to the world': Kovesi, p. 313.

'Of course the only thing that will have to happen is that Abbotsford will have to go'; 'I was just, oh, breathless because Abbotsford had … And I thought: "Oh, how could you say such a thing?"': Kovesi, p. 311.

'There is no need to mention the sadness that filled the hearts … and how many of the latter passed from Abbotsford to their heavenly home': Kovesi, p. 325.

'great care of the slate tiles from the roof, which … superb workmanship and by now very valuable': Kovesi, p. 328.

Chapter 17—A gem

'The St Heliers site … cultural purpose': *Amendment No. L83, Yarra planning scheme: former Convent of the Sisters of the Good Shepherd, St Heliers site, Abbotsford: Report of a Panel and Advisory Committee pursuant to sections 151, 153, 155 and 157 of the Act / Panel and Advisory Committee: Kathryn Mitchell, Jeff Lodge, Henry Turnbull, 1999.*

'The convent part … for the people of Victoria': *Amendment No. L83, Report of a Panel and Advisory Committee, 1999.*

'The St Heliers site … visible, proud and certain': *Amendment No. L83, Report of a Panel and Advisory Committee, 1999.*

'Australand's plans … among the heritage buildings': Alison Dean, 'Convent ruling riles builders', *Melbourne Times*, 30 June 1999.

'We've already been through a long and exhaustive consultative … preferred the panel to make the hard decisions now': Alison Dean, 'Convent ruling riles builders', *Melbourne Times*, 30 June 1999.

Chapter 18—Everything you wanted

'as a gift … to our children and grandchildren': Premier Steve Bracks, 'St Helier's Convent saved for future generations', Office of the Premier media release, 12 June 2001.

Chapter 19—Saved

'This is the missing piece … long and hard for': 'Confirmation at last for old convent', *The Age*, 9 July 2005.

'The unique rural setting … for all Victorians': 'Confirmation at last for old convent', *The Age*, 9 July 2005.

'There is every sign … hard not to be hopeful': 'The battlers who refused to compromise', *The Age*, 7 September 2005.

'This means the future of the farm is secure, and we can grow and prosper': 'Confirmation at last for old convent', *The Age*, 9 July 2005.

'a victory for the people of Melbourne'; 'through sheer grit and determination': author interview with Patricia O'Donnell, 2018.

'The various celebrations … around anymore': 'Confirmation at last for old convent', *The Age*, 9 July 2005.

Chapter 20—Open

'heritage headache': *The Age*, 7 September 2005.

Index

THE MIEGUNYAH PRESS

This book was designed by Patrick Cannon
The text was typeset by Patrick Cannon
The text was set in 11 point New Caledonia with 15 points of leading
The text is printed on 70gsm Classic White
This book was edited by Katie Purvis

THE
MIEGUNYAH
PRESS